WHY DO WE HURT OURSELVES?

WHY DO WE
HURT OURSELVES?

*Understanding Self-Harm
in Social Life*

Baptiste Brossard

Indiana University Press

Bloomington and Indianapolis

This book is a publication of

Indiana University Press
Office of Scholarly Publishing
Herman B Wells Library 350
1320 East 10th Street
Bloomington, Indiana 47405 USA

iupress.indiana.edu

The paper used in this publication meets the minimum require-
ments of the American National Standard for Information
Sciences—Permanence of Paper for Printed Library Materials,
ANSI Z39.48–1992.

Translation by Baptiste Brossard and Rohan Todd.

Cataloging information is available from the Library of Congress.

ISBN 978-0-253-03639-1 (cloth)

ISBN 978-0-253-03640-7 (paperback)

ISBN 978-0-253-03641-4 (ebook)

1 2 3 4 5   23 22 21 20 19 18

Contents

Introduction

I$_{N}$ 1998, DURING an interview given to *Le Monde Diplomatique*, Pierre Bourdieu expressed some astonishment: "I have never ceased to be surprised by what might be called the paradox of *doxa*: the fact that the world order as it is, with its one-way streets and no-entry signs, both literally and figuratively, its obligations and its sanctions, is roughly respected; that there are no more transgressions and subversions, no more offences and follies." He opens a parenthesis: "One only has to look at the extraordinary agreement of the thousands of dispositions—or wills—required for five minutes of car traffic on the Place de la Bastille or that of the Concorde in Paris."[1]

There is a backstage to this convergence of practical senses. When caught in the motorized anarchy of large urban roundabouts, every driver knows that they must *take on themselves*. This expression speaks for itself. For all these vehicles to reach their destination, the drivers must undertake multiple small actions in order to manage the proliferation of constraints. One driver might listen to music, sometimes singing and bobbing along to it. Another bites his nails, grips the gearshift, or chews his lips. A woman clenches her fists on the steering wheel or taps nervously on the dashboard, smoking cigarette after cigarette. Others will only sense slight physical signs of concentration. We could extend this painting infinitely, but the crucial point is that these actions are undertaken by these drivers to manage themselves, rather than to manage each other.

This metaphor tells us about a dimension of social life observed by sociologists such as Norbert Elias or Erving Goffman: it illustrates how social order presupposes manifold microtechniques of power over oneself that facilitate interaction management. One controls oneself to preserve one's daily life, to assume relationships with others. In this way, by a sort of emotional conformism, we instinctively reproduce social norms that are originally imposed from the outside. And certain aggressive practices against oneself, far from transgressing this order, manifest—strikingly—its internalization.

This book deals with one of these practices, "self-injury": cutting, burning, beating oneself, once a day, once a week, once a month, or more. In our contemporary societies, this is the method used by some to relieve themselves of the tensions that punctuate their daily life, to carry their personal history, and/or to express a "malaise" that only a physical injury seems to alleviate, if only momentarily. This is a way in which we could quickly present this enigmatic practice.

How can we understand that some people, in the course of their trajectories, are led to injure themselves? The answer I give to this question is based on two simple epistemological principles. The first consists in saying that studying a behavior requires paying attention to its practical, concrete dimensions.[2] How are self-inflicted wounds practiced in situation? What are they *for* in everyday life? In what material contexts do they occur? In other words, this book does not aim to analyze the social significance of self-harm or its symbolic meaning in the West, cultural considerations some may expect from a sociologist. Rather its aim is to analyze the specific configurations surrounding, if not producing, the very acts of self-harming.

The second principle derives from the first: we cannot judge whether a practice is *in essence* good or bad for individuals, whether it is "normal" or "pathological," or whether it constitutes a so-called mental health problem; this is not to deny, of course, the suffering of self-injurers. Often, psychiatrists and psychologists who study self-harm, or any other socially considered pathological behavior, relate this behavior to what they identify as harmful. Everything happens, then, as if only the pathological could explain the pathological. These preconceptions must be ruled out, especially because the conclusions emerging from them are constantly outdated, since the boundary between the normal and the pathological varies from one society to another, from one period of history to another. Only a century ago, somnambulism was an occult manifestation. Fifty years ago, homosexuality was a mental illness. There is therefore no reason to suppose that a fundamentally specific interpretation model is necessary to understand the behaviors considered a mental health problem today. I will study the practice of self-injuring like any other practice, playing tennis or jogging, eating chocolate or working.

This approach lessens the sensational aspect of the studied phenomenon (blood, pain, madness, etc.) in favor of a more materialistic horizon. Like any practice, self-injury is part of the daily lives of the people involved. It therefore engages their position in the social world: their age, their social backgrounds, their gender, and so forth. From there, it is embedded into the history of socially constructed relationships with their relatives, friends, colleagues, or classmates. In short, this book defends a sociological and empirical approach to self-injury.

What Is Self-Injury?

When I talk about my research to people around me, they will often describe certain practices, such as crushing a cigarette on one's arm, before asking me, "So, is *that* self-injury?" There is clearly no definitive criteria specifying, once and for all, the practice of self-injury. Some medical publications suggest that this behavior is a syndrome, the natural traits of which can be identified in the same way that biologists discover a new molecule. As Peter Steggals puts it, they approach self-injury as a "thing."[3] But what is identified as self-injury is only a more or less arbitrarily defined category in the wide range of existing self-aggressive behaviors, that include activities as diverse as nail-biting, self-amputation, or tattooing.

In order to "limit the field of observation," to take Marcel Mauss's[4] formula, I have defined self-injury as follows:

- *It is an activity consisting of injuring oneself.* Qualifying self-injury as an activity may seem obvious, but this makes it clear that we speak of a type of practice and not of a type of person.
- *It is intentional.* The intentionality criterion distinguishes intentional self-harming, on the one hand, from more common acts such as nail-biting or smoking cigarettes, which are attacks on the body but whose motive is not, strictly speaking, the attack of the body and, on the other hand, from so-called stereotypical self-injuries,[5] performed compulsively, without intention.
- *It occurs regularly.* The repetitiveness criterion differentiates what I call self-injury from other punctual conducts, such as, for example, someone who might punch a wall because they were upset that day. It also suggests a physical gravity criterion, because for a type of injury to repeat, it must not be definitive. In other words, it is not a self-amputation.
- *It is without deliberate suicidal intention.* The injury is performed without the will to commit suicide, although it is often observed that people who self-injure attempt suicide more often than the general population.[6]
- *There is no deliberately aesthetic or sexual intent.* This criterion distinguishes self-injury from many behaviors involving injuring one's

body performed for other reasons, especially (sado)masochism and body art.

- *It is without social recognition.* To my knowledge, no group explicitly values this practice, except perhaps the members of a few English-speaking internet forums. This criterion also makes it possible to distinguish the self-mutilations of adolescents and young adults from the scarifications related to rites of passage in other societies.

I will therefore define "self-injury," as well as the closely related, though not synonymous, terms "self-harm" and "self-wounding," as an activity consisting of injuring oneself, intentionally and repeatedly, without deliberate suicidal, aesthetic, or sexual intent, and without social recognition. This definition excludes a range of behaviors, for example, attempted suicides, sexual sadomasochism, or aesthetic scarification.

Some Figures

It remains difficult to measure the spread of this practice. The available statistical surveys are not all based on the same definitions. For example, on one hand, some include suicide attempts while others do not. On the other hand, the social stigma surrounding self-injury suggests significant biases in the responses to surveys: some people probably prefer to not report this behavior, even before an anonymous interviewer. In particular, surveys among the "general" population should be addressed with special consideration.

In various western geographic areas, it is estimated that around 5 percent of the general population have injured themselves, while this proportion is higher for adolescents, around 15 percent, and the lifetime prevalence increases to 18 percent.[7] Studies have estimated that the average age of first injury in North America is fifteen.[8] There seems to be a greater proportion of women involved, although researchers are not unanimous on this matter.[9]

Unfortunately, there is little to no information regarding the socio-economic background of self-injurers. Most research in this realm is carried out by psychologists or epidemiologists for whom this variable is not significant. Nonetheless, some works suggest that self-injurers are "typically an intelligent adolescent middle- or upper-class female."[10]

Most psychiatrists have also observed an increase in self-injury among their patients since the 1990s, some going so far as to label it an epidemic. Patricia and Peter Adler argue that the mid-1990s is a pivotal period, because of the growing media visibility of self-injury in the United States at that time.[11] Self-injury has attracted increased attention in the medical world since the 1990s: the first psychiatric publications dealing specifically with superficial self-injury (in opposition to self-amputations) appeared in the 1990s in the Francophone world while some Anglophone publications on the subject emerged as early as the 1960s.[12]

The hypothesis of proliferation of self-injury is not supported by any tangible quantitative evidence. There are almost no longitudinal studies on the subject, and comparing several surveys from different time periods is not viable, mainly because self-harm is defined in different ways in each survey. Regular monitoring of self-injury cases in Oxford hospitals between 1990 and 2000 concluded that self-injury increased. Unfortunately, this research does not differentiate self-injury from suicide attempts. To further complicate matters, meta-analysis of statistical surveys found a stabilization of prevalence rates since 2005.[13] Moreover, the difficulty of distinguishing a real increase in self-harming from an increase in reporting by patients or doctors remains. In the rush of emergency services, these behaviors might also be recorded as domestic accidents.

In contrast, there is an apparently demonstrable risk of "contagion" within psychiatric units. Two studies, one in the United States and the other in Finland, estimate that self-injuries are "grouped" around the same periods, suggesting a mimetic effect among patients.[14] A Canadian survey shows that, among those who have never self-injured, long-term psychiatric hospital stays do not influence the emergence of self-injurious behaviors. Yet hospitalization facilitates such behaviors among patients who have previously self-injured.[15] These statistical studies are consistent with the observations of some psychiatrists.[16] More studies would be needed to reach a conclusion.

Investigating a Discreet Practice

We are dealing with the practice of a minor, but nonetheless significant, set of people. How, then, to study it? By meeting with people who self-injure, or who have self-injured in the past, and conducting interviews with them, I have inquired into how their self-aggressive practices occur, or occurred, and into their history more generally.

Early in my research, a particular difficulty became apparent. Self-injury has no place. If I had wanted to write a book on golf, I would have gone to a golf course to meet with golfers. But this is not possible with self-injury, especially since this behavior is experienced as intimate and, hence, often hidden from the eyes of others. In order to overcome this difficulty, I chose two types of places where I might encounter people who self-injure. I met a large number of the participants on internet forums specifically devoted to self-injury, and I underwent traineeships in two mental health facilities for teenagers.

On the Internet

Using the internet as the frame of a sociological survey was a relatively untapped opportunity when I started this work in 2006. It became apparent that, apart from a few technical details, it was possible for one to maintain the same posture online as for an ordinary off-line ethnographic survey. It was still possible to get in contact with people through their network of acquaintances, to frequent this network over a long period, to restore the context that presides over the production of the respondents' narratives, and so forth. Adapting ethnographic methods in an online context was all the more necessary considering that, with the expansion of the internet since the 1990s, emerging communication media (discussion forums, chat rooms, instant messaging, etc.) were becoming increasingly commonplace in the daily lives of young people, adolescents, and also adults. Moreover, intimate, stigmatized, secretive behavior has gradually become visible online.[17] So, it made sense to look at the internet. A researcher must know how to adopt the techniques and communication codes of his participants, in the same way that an ethnologist working in a given territory must learn the language commonly spoken there.

However, the internet is an immense territory, too immense to investigate. I concentrated on French-speaking discussion forums devoted to self-injury, of which there were four at the time. With a few variations, they all aim to enable exchange of ideas about self-harm, and to encourage their members to support each other in facing the emotions that engender and result from self-injury. They are called "mutual aid" spaces.

After first contacting the administrators of these sites, and conducting interviews with them when possible, I proceeded by using networks of acquaintances, otherwise known as "the snowball technique." This entailed asking each participant to introduce me to some of their friends on the forum, and then asking this friend to recommend me to others, and so on.[18] I also posted a message on the forums, asking for people to interview.

In doing so, I met with forty-two people, mainly from two forums. I conducted face-to-face or instant-messaging interviews with them, and in some cases both. The interviews were supplemented by more informal conversations and other documents, such as autobiographical texts published on blogs or books, some of which were published (in fact, two participants published autobiographies). In addition to this are the readable narratives on the studied forums and the regular observation of these spaces online between 2006 and 2010, which also contributed to the data collected.

Interviews with internet users may be described as taking-stock interviews. From what I understood and sometimes directly heard, talking to a sociologist was an opportunity for the participants to experience an unusual interaction with the potential to enrich their self-reflection. As in the forums, the interviewees intended to "take stock" of their practice and their life at large. Moreover, for those who sought to quit self-injury, participating in the interviews entailed the prolongation of a reflexive posture.

Into Hospitals

Other interviews were conducted with adolescents and young adults hospitalized in two psychiatric institutions: the first, a day hospital for teenagers in a relatively wealthy suburb of the Paris region, and the second, a closed unit for suicidal teenagers in a provincial city.

A day hospital is an institution where patients go during the day for therapeutic activities, to receive their medication, and to attend to the planned consultations with psychiatrists or psychologists. Patients to not reside at the day hospital but go home at night and on weekends. Consequently, these institutions welcome relatively stabilized patients. I was admitted as a sociologist trainee in one of these services offered at the hospital, which has the peculiarity of including an integrated high school. Patients can continue their education with specialized teachers and schedules. Most of the patients were adolescents and were hospitalized for eating disorders, suicidal ideation, school phobias, and sometimes schizophrenia. Some of the patients had self-injured in the past. Working with the healthcare team, I participated in some activities and took advantage of any free time to conduct interviews with patients.

The patients accepted my request partly because they wanted the interview to help them in "taking stock," in the same way internet users did. In an institution where they are constantly encouraged to talk about themselves, the opportunity of talking to a sociologist—that is, in a new interaction frame—seemed to intrigue patients enough to make them open to the interviews. But my position as a trainee involved a greater degree of formality than with the participants encountered on the internet. The employment of formal language, in particular the use of *vous* (a formal way of saying "you" in French), created distance and reaffirmed affiliation with the caregivers. More importantly, from the moment a patient committed to an interview, they were obliged to come. The appointment then became one of their obligations to be present and to participate in the life of the facility, and its scheduling was often displayed on the same information board where the consultations were. A refusal to come might have worked against the patients as an indication of therapeutic ill will.

The situation was quite different in the other hospital I worked at, also as a sociologist trainee. This time, my interventions were not integrated into everyday activities. I only attended the team meetings to get acquainted with the patients' situations before conducting interviews with them. The service was a closed unit, welcoming teenagers who had made suicide attempts and/or had plausibly threatened to end their lives. Patients slept at the facility and their movements were strictly controlled by professionals. Unlike the day hospital where hospitalizations were rather long—usually several months, or even several years—these were emergency hospitalizations. Admitted adolescents were expected to stay for a maximum of two weeks before being moved elsewhere. More than half of the patients self-injured in the twelve-bed facility. They agreed to an interview very easily. Indeed, in a closed hospital, people are very bored. Any activity is good to join as long as it breaks the slow routine of hospitalization. Most patients agreed to talk to me before I could even finish explaining the aim of my research.

The Interviewing Process

I thus asked the interviewees to give me an interview, that is, a conversation, more or less formalized and recorded, during which I encouraged them to tell me their history, especially anything that concerned self-injury. The interviews were semistructured and organized around a list of topics to be broached. The participants were invited to develop these topics, using my questions as prompts to explore any related themes. Topics for discussion included descriptions of self-aggressive behaviors, the assumed causes of self-injury, social and family situations, school life and various activities (leisure, sports, and cultural practices), internet use, friends, romantic life, and care path. These themes were discussed during the course of the conversation, according to the associations of ideas made by the participants. Before recording the interviews, I presented the research and the rules of confidentiality. In order to ensure the confidentiality of the results, the names of places and persons have been modified.

With participants met on the internet, the recordings lasted between one and one and a half hours, which is rather short. Given the seriousness of some of the topics discussed, and the fatigue caused by their evocation, I preferred setting up another date rather than persevering. The talk time was even shorter with hospital patients, lasting between half an hour and an hour. Here, the time limit was affected by their ability to concentrate, which, in some cases, was altered by their emotional state or by medication.

Generally, the relations between the participants and myself could be characterized as friendly. I wanted to give the interviews an informal aspect to alleviate the discomfort that usually occurs at the beginning of such conversations, and because the interviews dealt with intimate topics. Besides the recorded conversations, I was able to stay in touch with some of the participants under more informal conditions, via instant messaging, by telephone, and through face-to-face conversations conducted in cafes, which allowed me to obtain further information.

During the interviews, refusal to address certain topics considered too painful or intimate was rare. Sometimes I perceived signs of subtle unwillingness, which tested my ability to distinguish between simple embarrassment and outright disinclination. Some participants refused to do a second or third interview, indicating an attempt to cut themselves off from anything that, from near or far, would make them think of self-injury. These reactions emphasize the significance of accepting a request for an interview. An interview is not just a discussion, it also amounts to accepting a link with self-injury.

In sum, I gathered narratives from sixty-eight people who self-injured at some point in their lives. It is worth considering how the method of recruiting participants might have partly influenced the proposed analysis, because it might have encouraged a certain type of person to participate. As most of the participants were internet users integrated into mutual-help forums for a long time, many provided positive feedback regarding these online spaces. Some self-injurers, though, reported that they had attempted to join such communities but did not find them beneficial. Since the potential participants were asked to talk about themselves and self-injury, it may have fostered the contribution of people who were in a process of distancing themselves from this practice (and many were quitting or had quit when I met them), and who "went far" in self-aggressive behaviors. As outlined in my introductory post in the forums, my association with an academic institution may have encouraged the participation of those who experienced a certain relationship with education or with the university more broadly.

But this research is qualitative, which means that the representation of the sample is not a key issue. An investigation consisting of sixty-eight participants is never really going to be representative of the general population, let alone a population as large as self-injurers. Rather, the purpose of this study is to gain an in-depth understanding of the general, social dynamics underlying narratives of self-harm, and more than a method of collecting data, to propose a method of analysis aimed at reaching these dynamics beyond the particular stories collected.

The Social Conditions of Self-Injury

Let us be more specific: what can these narratives teach us about self-harm? Can they aid in discovering some causes? To find and identify factors? To deduce explanations and make interpretations? I don't think so. However, we can derive a set of social conditions from the data. Here's why.

An interview is a singular interaction, in which a person stages oneself and tells what they want to tell in the way that suits them, or at least in a way that they have worked through in previous interactions. For example, the participants involved in internet forums had already shaped their biographical narrative through talking to other forum members. Pierre Bourdieu has developed the notion of biographical illusion to suggest that, even unconsciously, our narratives about ourselves are being reformulated and elaborated at each enunciation.[19] We do not make identical statements about our histories when we are twenty, forty, or sixty years old, and our statements deviate according to whether we are in front of an audience, our parents, or a close friend. The interviews I have conducted, though certainly based on facts, are interpretations that are more or less consciously reformulated within the interaction. The point is not to assert that these narratives may have no value but that their analysis requires some caution. First of all, the challenge is to present these narratives with a degree of distance from the positions expressed in them. To ensure this distance, I have sought throughout the book to clarify where I am citing interview extracts and where I am elucidating the finding of my research; to distinguish between their accounts and mine. And, when presenting the narratives of the participants, I have tried to maintain a distance toward them, not expressing my opinion and values regarding what they were recounting, suggesting enough to doubt. Second, the status granted to these narratives must be clarified.

In the first part of this book, I rely on the participants' descriptions of their self-aggressive practices. The result is a detailed presentation of these behaviors that seeks to locate them broadly within the individual's trajectories and, more specifically, within the particular immediate contexts in which they occur, including the time of day or moment of injury. This part shows, among other things, that self-injury is a practice that people use to *self-control*—to calm down, or to avoid "going haywire" or "breaking everything"—and thus to maintain the interaction order. The analysis is based mainly on the fact that the narratives gathered have a collective dimension, insofar as common points emerge from them. Indeed, these narratives allow us to observe experiences that overlap and look alike. All the participants, even when they did not know each other, described similar processes of action, a feature that recalls a genuine Durkheimian social fact.

I follow a different mode of analysis in the second part of the book. During the interviews, the interviewees spoke of the reasons that apparently led them to self-injury and, more generally, to feeling bad. These reasons mainly consist of accusations regarding their family situation (such as not getting along with parents) or striking events such as sexual abuse. Faced with these accusations, I selected some particularly eloquent stories as illustrations, in order to propose a method of analyzing self-harm as a practice of social positioning. Indeed, we will see that through these behaviors and the associated narratives, individuals express a positioning (rejection or attraction) vis-à-vis people around them, people who embody specific social positions, in terms of class, gender, age, and their social trajectory in general. In this part, I will openly rely on the participants' subjective accounts and take distance from these accounts by analyzing them within a general sociological framework.

These two modes of analysis will lead me to identify some social conditions of self-injury. By this expression, I wish to convey that simple causal relationships cannot be mobilized to explain any behavior, such as "X causes self-injury." This is a problematic logic that we often hear regarding traumas suspected of causing self-injury. The expression "social conditions" also makes it possible to consider that certain aspects of the life of individuals (biographical events, family configuration, relationship to the body, etc.) have triggered the *possibility* of self-injuring, without necessarily *leading* to it. The relationship between the conclusions reached in each part of this book is not intended to be understood as implying a direct causal relation or as being accumulated factors. Instead, the conclusions drawn constitute some of the myriad conditions that lead more or less directly to self-harming.

In summary, some individuals (and not others), placed in some circumstances (and not others) and subjectively described during the interviews, self-injure. My purpose, then, is to understand under what conditions self-injury is actually practiced, and in so doing, to grasp the conditions by which some people are led to injure themselves.

Issues in Sociological Writing

How do we convey the findings of this research? With the present book, I have attempted to describe the results of my research in a manner that is both academically valid, in the sense that the methodology and theoretical grounding used reflect the state of current literature in sociology, and is readable by a wider, nonacademic audience. Consequently, I will not fully endorse the standard academic style, which prevails in contemporary scholarly publications and is characterized by a rigid mode of writing, saturated with citations and technical terms. I have attempted here to write in a more minimalist style, more common to nonacademic texts, without sacrificing any complexity in reasoning. For example, this entails citing only those publications necessary to understand the development of the argument I am proposing, rather than swamping the reader with extensive and tangentially relevant citations.

In addition to promoting a certain mode of sociological writing, this writing style allows me to devote greater space to the participants' stories. In this regard, closer to the ethnographic sensitivity, this book provides in-depth accounts of what the participant narrated. It aims to immerse the reader within the social situations under study. In other words, I do not want the reader to have only an accurate knowledge of my analysis but also of the biography and situations of the self-injurers discussed herein. This deviates from the dominant writing style, which privileges short excerpts of interviews, usually consisting of one or two sentences that *perfectly fit* with the analyses, thus showcasing *perfect* analyses. The long narratives presented have obviously been chosen because they illustrate my analysis. Importantly, though, they also reveal the complexity of the individual cases I have studied. This complexity may at times overflow the slick analysis one might expect of the researcher, encouraging a critical distance both from the conclusions and from the narratives of the participants.

Finally, interrogating sociological writing in this way leads me to address the issue of the monopolization of self-injury research by psychiatric discourses, and regarding mental health more broadly. Indeed, in a context where the "evidence-based medicine" dominates the subject of self-injury, developing an account that seeks to not only provide alternative, sociologically informed perspectives on self-injury but also to explore various ways of wording these perspectives is invaluable.

Here, the alternative proposed can be summarized as follows. Self-injury is not a matter of some "crazy" individuals who resort to self-injury in the face of individual weaknesses and difficulties. Rather, self-injury is a matter of the reactions of individuals to the tensions that compose, day after day, the tumultuousness of social life. To understand this, we need to explore in detail how social trajectories make self-injury a comprehensible and reasonable practice.

Part I
A Practice of Self-Control

Introduction

COMMON SENSE AND psychological literature apply many labels to self-injury. These labels plunge us into social imaginings that are more (or less) attractive by their marginality or their exoticism: craziness, adolescent suffering, suicide, initiation rituals, body art, mental disorders, or masochism. Ultimately though, self-injury is a practice; it is nothing more than an activity consisting of a set of repeated acts.

To study this practice, we must first describe how it occurs and trace the issues that the concerned individuals face. Their motivations to hurt themselves are embedded within the activities that make up their everyday lives. These activities produce the use of injuries, shape their practical modalities, elaborate the possibilities of saying or silencing them, and organize the conditions of their visibility. Such an examination, therefore, requires distinguishing three temporalities:

1. The longest of these temporalities is the trajectory of the participants: during a given period of their life, they injure themselves on a regular basis. In this context, self-injury becomes a biographical period in which several stages can be identified, from the first wound to the cessation. But why opt for this unusual term, "trajectory"? Simply put, it is a matter of theoretical coherence. Adopting an expression such as "career" puts emphasis on a group's influence on the evolution of the individual's behaviors, while in this study, the participants are mostly loners. Moreover, the expression "path," which might also be a suitable term, highlights the supposed freedom of an individual to "pursue their own path," which, sociologically speaking, is disputable. Among these expressions, "trajectory" seems to be the most adequate because it refers metaphorically to the navigator within social space, evoking the intertwining of individual orientations and the structural forces shaping them, namely, a matter of agency. Self-injury trajectories will be developed in the chapters 1, 2, 3, and 4.

3

2. The second temporality is composed of what we shall call the *self-injury process*. The *self-injury process* encompasses all significant interactions and moments that occur before an injury, which lead to and succeed the act of self-injury. This expression thus underscores that while, by definition, the act of injuring oneself is central to self-injury, self-injuring cannot be simply reduced to this act itself. This process will be recounted in chapter 5.

3. Finally, the smallest temporal scale is the act itself: the wounding, an act that may last a few seconds or minutes. In this scale, the practical modalities of the injury (i.e., the type of self-harm, the degree of ritualization) and the associated emotional system (i.e., the relationship between the emotion to be discarded and the emotion sought) all play an essential role. This temporality will be dealt with in chapter 6.

1   The First Time

UNDER WHAT CIRCUMSTANCES does the first injury occur?

This question falls within the sociological study of deviant behaviors, which, broadly defined, studies behaviors that are socially stigmatized because they transgress the norms of a social group. As Patricia and Peter Adler point out, self-injurers enter the two categories of lonely deviance developed by Joel Best and David Luckenbill: they are *loners*, given that they proceed without needing relations with similar others, and they are *individual deviants*, in that they engage in deviant activities by themselves.[1] Consequently, for the sociologist accustomed to initially looking at the impact of groups and institutions on individuals, this practice remains mysterious.

As Best and Luckenbill suggest, solitary deviants are thus socialized into their deviance by "society at large," rather than by supposedly deviant groups inaugurating a change in the individual's mindset toward norms. The first step to understanding this difference in the case of self-injury is to explore how the first instance of self-injury occurs, and this chapter will outline some analytical categories to account for it.

What Happened?

Many of the participants of this study expressed a haziness surrounding the first instance of self-injury. Judith, with whom I conducted several interviews, is exemplary of this:

> INTERVIEWER: Can you tell me when you started self-injuring?
>
> JUDITH: Uh ... I was in ninth grade, in fact ... honestly, it's a bit of a blur, how I started... It started ... Not much eh ... it was ... At first, I didn't even know what it was ... [*silence*]

Judith does not remember exactly what happened. Indeed, while most participants remember their first injury, many do not perceive a specific reason for the act. Even if a significant event occurs that provokes the urge to hurt oneself, the motivation, like the choice of this practice rather than another, is completely vague. There is no reason to assume that the attack of the body is, in itself, the motivation for this type of activity. On this point, I share David Grange's criticism against the teleological analyses of self-aggression: "behaviors such as bulimia/ anorexia, alcoholism, drug addiction, self-neglect ... have, in practice, a deleterious effect on the health of the person who does it.... It is a fact, but nothing indicates that this is their vocation."[2]

Understanding the first self-wound, and moreover the management of its enunciation in an interview situation, leads us to look into *a posteriori*—constructed explanations. Amandine was nineteen years old at the time of our discussion, in March 2008. This young Quebecois explains to me:

> [Instant messaging]
>
> AMANDINE: I started almost five years ago. I do not remember how the idea came to my mind, I grabbed a compass and engraved the word DEAD on my wrist ... without knowing what self-injury was.... I had great difficulties with my parents, I was in major suicidal depression, I went to PH [Psychiatric Hospital] for that and I went out ... I continued SI [Self-Injuring] after that....
>
> INTERVIEWER: Ok ... and you remember why you wanted to do it? Why the word "DEAD"?
>
> AMANDINE: Why I wanted to do it, in the beginning, I think, was to make a concrete gesture toward my death ... and the word "dead" because it was my goal ... later I made five suicide attempts.
>
> INTERVIEWER: It was like a kind of training?
>
> AMANDINE: No ... I don't remember exactly that time ... but I know that I quickly discovered the good it did ... I switched to cuts after, it was much more liberating than simple letters with the compass.

Unable to remember her precise motives, Amandine introduces an "I think" before "to make a concrete gesture toward my death." Here, we can perceive the influence of her studies in psychology on her narrative. This turn of phrase and the expression, "I was in major suicidal depression," recall how mental health professionals talk and their inclination to interpret actions through unconscious reasons. Moreover, Amandine's use of the expression, "I think, was to make a concrete gesture toward my death," means both that she has developed this interpretation retrospectively and that she feels as though unconscious motivations were at work.

The initial enigma persists: was the first injury a purely "spontaneous" act? The elusive origin of this act is even more troubling because the first time takes on a particular importance within the self-harming trajectory. From this initial act, individuals realize that this behavior provides them with relief, and a sense of dependence develops. Over time, self-injury becomes a motivation in itself. But how should we study the motivations of the first wound when the people concerned express difficulty discussing it?

The Study of Motives

Howard Becker writes about people entering deviant careers, stating that "people usually think of deviant acts as motivated. They believe that the person who commits a deviant act, even for the first time (and perhaps especially for the first time), does so purposely. His purpose may or may not be entirely conscious, but there is a motive force behind it."[3] This de facto situation is not confined to illegal or illegitimate acts. Who knows the true motives of their daily practices, if such motives exist at all? Who is *really* aware, for example, of the reasons driving their initial participation in a leisure activity or, for that matter, their involvement in a given professional sector?

We generally assume that when someone develops a deviant practice, they have justification for it, while simultaneously we share an ignorance toward the motivations of our own socially accepted activities. In this regard, the participants' narratives are likely to be much more elaborate than one given by an individual asked about a behavior deemed socially legitimate, such as playing ping-pong on a Sunday afternoon. Here, a justification by taste ("I like it") may appear to be sufficient. But because they are engaged in unusual behaviors, the people I met had already reflected on a way to justify their practice, prior to the interviews. They are somehow socially summoned to hold a reflexive posture toward their behavior.

Moreover, I believe that the more socially illegitimate a behavior is, the more that it is suspected to rely on deep, unconscious, and inaccessible motivations. In our case, this implies that the quest for a motivation regarding the first injury constitutes also, and perhaps above all, an expectation *toward* the self-injurers. Howard Becker has encouraged us to reverse these questions, suggesting that "instead of the deviant motives leading to the deviant behavior, it is the other way around; the deviant behavior in time produces the deviant motivation." In his seminal study of marijuana smokers, Becker showed how "vague impulses and desires ... are transformed into definite patterns of action through the social interpretation of a physical experience which is in itself ambiguous."[4]

We will see that self-injurers also gradually *learn* to find a precise sensation in the wound, although this learning often happens alone. But there is another difference. Through the social imaginary surrounding its consumption, the marijuana smoker has an idea of the effect that the drug should produce. Except for a few participants who explained that they had begun self-injuring after observing the relief that people around them seemed to gain from it, the motivating effects of self-injury are often unknown before the first wound.

The issue of motivation, even in Becker's writing, is in fact too narrowly considered. In his study of marijuana smokers, he focuses on the longing to smoke marijuana or to socialize in a group of smokers. These motives are all directly related to drugs, whereas one can imagine someone starting to smoke for other reasons, such as escaping a social, familial, or emotional situation, or desiring to improve one's popularity among school peers, including nonsmokers. We should not assume that only the content of a deviant behavior plays as a potential motivation for this behavior.

To avoid this difficulty, it is sufficient to consider that the first time is a biographical moment. In this context, the first injury becomes the intersection, at a given time, of an intention, a circumstance, and a biographical passage. The "intention" refers to the conscious motive expressed by the participant about this first self-injury (motivation, as we have said, is often insufficiently developed in the interviews). By "circumstance," I mean the material framework of the wound, namely the place, the time of day, and the interactions preceding the act. Finally, the "biographical passage" describes the participants' situation at this point in their lives, their preoccupations, their family and school situation, the events that they find significant, and so on.

An Intention, a Circumstance, a Biographical Passage

Let us take the example of Beatrix, a fourteen-year-old high school student in the tenth grade. She also expresses the haziness surrounding the reasons underlying her first injury. Nonetheless, she remembers its circumstances:

[Instant messaging]

INTERVIEWER: So, can you tell me when you started to self-injure? How did it happen?

BEATRIX: On a Thursday. Half the class had gone skiing, and it was a day of strike action, so I had not gone to school. A banal day. I had nothing to do.

Without acknowledging any motive, Beatrix finds herself in a situation of loneliness—which, as we shall see, often favors the recourse to self-injury—and in a biographical moment, characterized by the recent death of her father coupled with difficulties with friends. Solitude leads her to revisit her past. In other words, the circumstance in which she finds herself (solitude) momentarily reinforces the impact of her biographical passage (the death of her father).

For Lisa, a nineteen-year-old high school student in vocational training, the configuration looks similar:

[Instant messaging]

LISA: I do not remember exactly when it was. In the year when I turned fourteen, I walked out of my home, and I started at that time. I settled outside and I saw a piece of glass. After I don't remember what pushed me to take it, but it started like that, then I kept doing it.

INTERVIEWER: Why did you leave your house?

LISA: After a fight with my mother, now it seems stupid for me to have left for that, but at the time… I have very conflicting relations with my mother.

Like Beatrix, Lisa does not identify any particular intention in her act, but she is able to clearly identify its circumstance as well as the biographical moment. Lisa says that she had been assaulted when she was eleven, and had only told her parents three years afterward. She did not wish to specify the type of assault. After this announcement, her parents seemed distraught and sought to "know everything," which, according to Lisa, resulted in many family tensions.

The intention of the first self-injury is clearer in the cases where the participants injure themselves in preparation for suicide, as a manner of training, or at least as a means to symbolically approach a more-or-less desired death. This is what Louise, a twenty-two-year-old literature student, narrates:

> [Instant messaging]
>
> INTERVIEWER: The first time, you remember?
>
> LOUISE: Yes, very well.
>
> I wanted to die
>
> I wanted to open my veins, but it was very superficial.
>
> But I noticed that hurting myself relieved me, so I did it again.

Despite these exceptions, the motive of the first wound generally remains mysterious, whereas the circumstance and the biographical passage are more easily recounted. The gap between a difficult-to-describe intention and an easily identified context helps us understand the mechanism at work in the first time. From this, we can indeed understand that when facing a "trouble,"[5] a malaise, some uncertainty exists regarding the possible behaviors to adopt. The participants often give the impression of having reacted as best they could, of having done something just to do something. The first injury may thus be described as a form of "spontaneous" expression, but not according to the common usage of this adjective. It is an act whose initial intention is neither formulated nor rationalized by the one who performs it, and thus it is consequently experienced as spontaneous.

Are There Predispositions?

The idea to self-injure in the face of a problem does not immediately occur to everyone. For this possibility to emerge spontaneously there must first be a familiarity with self-aggression so that the self-inflicted wound appears as a possible form of spontaneous expression. Many participants described their first-time self-injuring as part of behaviors or desires that had animated them for a while. Are we to attribute this to biographical reconstruction or reality? We cannot know. Nevertheless, it is the first possibility—biographical reconstruction—that is necessary to perceive oneself as someone who *may* self-injure.

Camille, a twenty-three-year-old literature student, explains that self-injury refers to the behaviors that have shaped her relationship with emotions since childhood:

[Face to face]

CAMILLE: I don't really know when I started, I really began self-injuring like that ... that is, the cutter in the arm, I think I was about fifteen or sixteen. But I had ... I mean it was dormant, it was going to happen. Let's say I don't believe that someone who is totally normal can see someone else self-injuring and tell himself, "Well, what if I do that myself?" and start self-injuring. Let's not be dumb. I mean ... I remember very well that around ten or twelve, I spent winter nights, when it was cold, with only a T-shirt and underwear at the edge of the window ... because I couldn't sleep if I wasn't cold enough. Yes, behaviors like that ... behaviors like when there is something that gets on your nerves, you hit the walls, you kick it, it hurts but for you it lets off steam, stuff like that. Then, you set the limit of what self-injury is or what it is not.

INTERVIEWER: Before you self-injured, where did these behaviors come from?

CAMILLE: No idea. My character, I imagine. Uh, for me it was the reaction to have, I never thought of it especially. For example, nobody has ever prevented me from talking about my problems or whatever. I just never did.

For the most part, participants describe the gradual emergence of a feeling of strangeness, of abnormality. Patricia and Peter Adler report the same type of feeling among some of their informants.[6] Camille says it well: "I don't believe that someone who is totally normal can see someone else self-injuring and tell himself, 'well, what if I do that myself?'" The question is not whether an individual is normal or not, but whether that individual is able to perceive themselves, beforehand, as a person abnormal enough to enable this kind of deviance. In this regard, the biographical illusion becomes performative.

In his research on marijuana smokers, Howard Becker provides an uncompromising critique of theories that attempt to explain the entry into deviant careers in terms of individual predispositions. He attacks the psychological, even neurological, models against which he seeks to substitute his own. Becker's model, on the contrary, consists in showing the emergence of deviant motives due to the socialization within a deviant group. To do so, he implicitly assumes that a predisposition leading to smoking marijuana would be a predisposition to only smoke marijuana. However, from a sociological perspective, the predisposition to enter a deviant career could be understood as the self-persuasion that a predisposition toward deviant behavior exists. In other words, a predisposition to smoke marijuana or self-injure need not result from a motivation toward engaging in these specific actions, but rather toward acting in a deviant manner in general. Many participants thus expressed having for a long time (or even always) felt "apart," or "a little bit different."

Another type of social predisposition stems from a reduction in the degree of illegitimacy regarding certain deviances through socialization. Élodie, a twenty-three-year-old student working toward an associate's degree in commerce, illustrates this. She says that she no longer knows exactly when her self-injury started, but explains that getting hurt has been a "mode of expression" (she puts it in quotation marks on *MSN Messenger*) since childhood. She tied her practice to the education provided by her parents. Élodie explains that her parents did not hesitate to resort to physical punishment. Integrating a principle of aggression from her childhood may lead, logically, to a *performative* predisposition toward self-aggressive behaviors, insofar as it can be assumed that this type of socialization makes it easier to envisage any form of (self) aggression.

This set of remarks constitutes a potential way out of the questions raised in sociological literature regarding whether self-injury would be "self-learned" or "other-learned."[7] Self-injury is not necessarily learned directly within a group (as in Becker's work) or through exposure to a media. However, this does not exclude the possibility that it is *socially learned* in other, indirect ways, as Best and Luckenbill suggest regarding solitary deviances.

Self-Injury Among Other Practices

The previous question hides another one. Defining self-injury as a coherent set of behaviors should not lead to an ossification of this definition, which would entail isolating self-injury from other possible self-aggressive practices. In some cases, the premises of self-injury manifest in the form of a priori "close" activities. Amy Chandler relates the same process. The participants in her study distinguish self-injury from previous self-injurious behaviors and trace the premises of their behaviors back to childhood, which Chandler interprets as a means to embed self-injury in their "authentic self."[8] The presentation that Antoine, a twenty-six-year-old master's student in building construction, makes of his trajectory illustrates a certain porous quality of the practices. When I ask him to date all the self-aggressive behaviors that he has had, he answers:

[Instant messaging]

ANTOINE: Going out in a T-Shirt (in winter), from sixteen to twenty-one years old (but with time it doesn't even burn anymore), sixteen years old, cuts, like two or three, eighteen years old, punches (not many, four or five times in one year, at most), nineteen/twenty years old … cuts (maybe twice), blows; I was containing myself, but maybe once a week at certain times, usually at least, it's extremely complicated, I've burnt myself twice, and mental SI [Self-Injury] … and I'll have to explain what mental SI is (which is not real according to many, but which is real according to me)

INTERVIEWER: Yes, what do you call mental SI?

ANTOINE: Mental SI (personal definition, I do not know if the term exists); to hurt oneself, to destroy oneself, morally. Like watching disgusting porn movies while disgusting oneself of being a man, or, like a friend of mine, sleeping with the first guy coming along when we are a victim of sexual abuse disgusted by sex.

I frequently observed an alternating between eating disorders and self-mutilation. After an anorexic period culminated in hospitalization in a psychiatric institute, twenty-one-year-old Katie, began to self-injure by cutting herself when leaving the hospital. For Katie, these cuts are a means of daily self-control to avoid "becoming anorexic again." They act as a substitute. Maya, a nineteen-year-old sociology student, follows the opposite path. She became anorexic after a "takeover,"[9] which allowed her to stop self-injuring.

Various participants described the emergence of more common practices as a means of continuing self-harm. "Mental SI," as described by Antoine, a symbolic undertaking of self-degradation, can be found in a less-formalized form in many interviews. Thus Annabelle, a thirty-year-old computer scientist, reinterprets her emotional life through the prism of her self-aggressive behaviors.

[Face to face]

INTERVIEWER: In what context did you stop self-injuring the second time? You told me that it was during the second year of college ...

ANNABELLE: Uh ... why I stopped ... because, at the time, I already had seriously questioned myself.... Then because at the time I had found a boyfriend, but ... in a way, it hurt me more than if I would hurt myself.

INTERVIEWER: To have a boyfriend?

ANNABELLE: Yes ... because he was someone who did not respect me at all. And anyway, as I did not respect myself either, as I did not love myself, this [situation] did not bother me.

All this means that the very notion of a first time must be put in perspective, for self-inflicted injuries often emerge while a process of bodily or symbolic self-degradation is already underway through other self-aggressive practices.

A Deviant Behavior without Deviant Group

In sum, the interactionist sociology of deviance usually explains how individuals enter a deviant career by the socialization into groups, which provide individuals with other mindsets and conducts alternative to dominant norms. However, this process is not the case here. Most participants started injuring themselves alone.

The issue, then, is to understand how the possibility of self-injury is made available to individuals, such that this practice may, thereafter, come to their mind. In other words, if undertaking unconventional behaviors depends on the "structure of occasions" surrounding the individual, of their "space of possibilities,"[10] we must examine how an individual finds the *possibility* of self-harming. I have identified three mechanisms: innovation, importation, and imitation.

Innovation

Innovators are individuals who began to hurt themselves without the slightest idea that this behavior existed among other people. It is therefore an innovation, in the sense that the practice is created and then added to their set of behavioral possibilities. Eva, a twenty-three-year-old ambulance attendant, falls within this category: "And this is when I ... I remember the first time ... I remember bumping my head and I remember, I was looking for something to cut myself, but I did not know what that was" [face to face].

The clearest innovation form manifests itself when the practice seems to emerge from nowhere. Eva gives the impression that she literally invented it, without "knowing what that was." This process is an instinctive experience. Consider, for example, Mathieu (an unemployed thirty-year-old communications and political science graduate) who talks about it in these terms: "One evening when I was not doing well, I had ... it seemed like a logical necessity."

This "logical necessity" often consists in radicalizing nervous childhood behaviors. Eighteen-year-old Noémie, who holds a technical school certificate in cuisine, thus explains the shift from the scratches she inflicted on herself in her most distant memories to her current self-injury, formalized by cuts:

[Face to face]

INTERVIEWER: So, you started self-injuring very young ...

NOÉMIE: Yes.

INTERVIEWER: And so you scratched yourself?

NOÉMIE: Yes, I was doing scratches, yes.

INTERVIEWER: When did you switch to cutting?

NOÉMIE: In sixth grade.

INTERVIEWER: What happened?

NOÉMIE: I was fed up ... scratches did not hurt enough anymore, that's all.

It would be difficult to say more, since memories dating back to childhood may give rise to profound reinterpretations and, more importantly, to a vagueness associated with the time separating the facts from the interview. The instability of childhood memories also suggests that among those whose description of self-injury fits the classification of "innovators" are those who we might deem "false innovators," in the sense that they have forgotten antecedent exposure to the self-injuries of others.

Importation

The motives of the first injury were rather obscure for the participants, except for those who planned to commit suicide. Stopping short of killing themselves, they become aware of the soothing virtues of the wound and continued to injure themselves. This type of entry into the self-injury trajectory can be qualified as an *importation*, insofar as self-injuries integrate with all the envisaged possibilities through another intention. This process resembles that of anorexic women, who begin their careers with a simple diet.[11] Annabelle recounts her first time: "So, I started at fifteen. Originally, in fact, we didn't really know that I was starting to be badly depressed, so I wanted to commit suicide, so I took some blades and wanted to see if they cut well. I notched myself just to see if it was fine, for the day I would end all this, and then a few days later I rechecked, and then again, and then I realized that it made me feel good, so I kept on going. I cut myself a lot for three years" [face to face]. The case of Clémence, a twenty-four-year-old master's student in sociology, is similar, except that her father's illness ultimately caused her to renounce suicide and retain only the habit of voluntary injury.

[Instant messaging]

INTERVIEWER: Can you tell me how you started to self-injure?

CLÉMENCE: I do not remember at all the first time.... I know it was a period when I was drinking a bit. A lot, actually.... In fact, it was more a training.

INTERVIEWER: A training?

CLÉMENCE: I planned to commit suicide actually ... for my birthday ... well, around that day. And suddenly, debauchery, before hitting a low point, so alcohol and everything.... Anyway, initially SI [Self-Injury], it was on the wrists and for training and then after that ... things became uncontrollable.

INTERVIEWER: Uncontrollable, in what sense?

CLÉMENCE: It's elsewhere [on the body], and SI for SI.

Interestingly, this type of entry into self-injury is consistent with the greater incidence of this behavior among young women. Statistically, women are more likely to commit suicide attempts than actual suicide, unlike men who report fewer attempts and more "successful" suicides.[12]

Other forms of importation exist, but they remain very rare. For example, Pascale began to hurt herself "as a game":

[Face to face]

INTERVIEWER: Can you tell me when you started hurting yourself?

PASCALE: Okay. So ... the very first time I did it, I was in eighth grade. So, it was a long time ago. I was in Spanish class, with a girlfriend at that time, we were sitting up front. And I was bored a lot, because I did not like Spanish very much. And I remember that I had a lot of small hair clips in my hair, that I removed a clip from my hair, that I took a pencil sharpener, that I put the clip in the pencil sharpener, that I took the clip from the pencil sharpener, and that I started playing with the blade of the pencil sharpener. And after a while, I put it on my hand, here [points to hand], and I cut myself. Without ... well, it was not bleeding. And my girlfriend almost died laughing, so I think I kept doing it because ... that's it. So, was it really to hurt me? I don't think so...

INTERVIEWER: Yeah, it was more to play ...

PASCALE: Yeah, it was more to play but anyway it's since then that it became ... from there it became ... after, I really did it to hurt myself though.

In fact, innovation and importation are very close processes since the will to commit suicide or self-injure "as a game" does not exclude the ignorance that self-mutilation is practiced by others. This is the case of Louise, who started self-injuring with a view toward committing suicide, but realized that the wounds relieved her. At that time, she thought that she was the only one engaging in this kind of behavior, before finding some information on the internet and learning that it is a rather widespread behavior among the juvenile population. Importation therefore consists of a form of innovation motivated at first by an intention other than bodily harm.

Imitation

Finally, imitators are individuals who draw inspiration from other self-injurers, and give it a try. They have an idea of the existence of this practice, having either seen scars on someone else, or spoken with someone about it. Benoît, a sixteen-year-old high school student, falls into this category: "I came to know [about SI] through my best friend who did it. I used to tell him 'you're so stupid, it's useless,' and all that . . . and that night, I could not calm down, I cried for an hour, and I had a cutter, and that's it" [face to face].

For Benoît, self-injury was incorporated into his behavioral possibilities prior to hurting himself, even if he was unable to grasp the appeal of this behavior for his friend. In other words, when he decided to try, he knew that this behavior was possible, without necessarily knowing why.

Occasionally, imitation results from direct incitement. This is the case of Marie, a fifteen-year-old eighth grade student: "I was with a friend . . . and we were talking . . . and I started to cry . . . well, I smoked, I started to cry . . . and I . . . actually she said 'ok, burn yourself, and maybe it'll be good for you,' and everything . . . and so, after, I burned myself, and I saw that it did me good so . . . I started again the next time" [face to face].

The entry of Vanessa, a twenty-three-year-old sociology student, into the trajectory of self-injury engages a more complex process. Here is an excerpt from her autobiographical text:

> Shortly before I turned seventeen, in December, during a day of boredom when I was alone at home, I was on the couch playing with sewing needles. I often slipped them under the superficial skin of my hands, as if it were a game. . . . This game reminded me that one year ago, at the usual ski camp, two girls, younger than me, had their arms wounded by parallel cuts. . . . I did not understand, despite the discussions with my friends, I did not know "what it was." . . . On that day, when I was playing with needles, I had the idea of going back to a website, a forum more precisely, which people visited, especially young people in the middle of teenager malaise, and mutilated themselves. Quite quickly it fascinated me, I discussed a little on the forum, and I started to do the same. It seemed to me a condition to be integrated on this forum.

This decision to self-injure consists of several steps: Vanessa began by "playing" with needles (which suggests an importation), then remembered having noticed scars on other people (which suggests an imitation), before expressing the desire to participate in the forum she visits online. Ultimately, the will to integrate into a group guides her initiative. However, it is worth noting that she is the only participant to evoke this type of motivation.

Cultural Productions: An Imitation Media?

This overview would not be complete without also considering the effect of more indirect mechanisms enabling individuals to discover the possibility of self-injury.

[Face to face]

INTERVIEWER: And your first self-injury dates back to when?

ANNE: April 2007.

INTERVIEWER: April 2007, ah, okay ...

ANNE: Yes, it was Monday, April 12th, around noon.

INTERVIEWER: And ... What happened on the 12th of April around noon?

ANNE: I was at the worst, I was lower than the ground, and I had to find a way, a way I don't know, I don't know and I thought about it, and I did it.

INTERVIEWER: Was there already someone who had done it around you?

ANNE: No.

INTERVIEWER: Did not you know it [SI] existed?

ANNE: I did not know that it existed, I didn't know that there were plenty of people who did this to get better, I didn't know at all, it was a reflex like that and that's it.

This excerpt from an interview with Anne, who was twenty-one years old at the time, would suggest that she is situated within the category of innovators. However, a little later in the conversation some remarks lead us to doubt this categorization.

[Face to face]

INTERVIEWER: And you watched movies maybe, dealing with self-injury?

ANNE: Yes.

INTERVIEWER: And what did you think?

ANNE: I loved it at first, I found myself in these characters, and then I think it's a good idea because it makes it possible to popularize self-harm, that way everyone knows what it is, because unfortunately there are still people who don't know what it is.

INTERVIEWER: What was the title?

ANNE: *Girl, Interrupted*, with Angelina Jolie, it's about a girl with borderline personality disorder, interned in a psychiatric hospital.

INTERVIEWER: And you recognized yourself ... in the main character?

ANNE: Yes.

INTERVIEWER: Okay, what did it evoke to you?

ANNE: The fact, I don't know.... It's a little difficult but the fact that she is ... that she is borderline, for example, nothing but that, and I recognized myself in her way of being.

Despite Anne's ability to date specific events in her life, she cannot remember whether she watched this film before or after her first injury. Based on the excerpt above, it appears that it was after. But—and this may apply to others—it is possible that viewing movies, series, documentaries, and reports, as well as reading novels or listening to radio programs, works as a source of information.

Nevertheless, all the people I interviewed during my research (except Anne and another respondent who changed her mind during the interview) said that the media did not influence them. Obviously, in an interview situation, this question places their image at risk by potentially insinuating that they are merely part of the mass of adolescents following the so-called fashion of self-injury, itself following all the caricatured cultural productions surrounding, for example, the Gothic movement. An image that is not very rewarding, a cliché perceived as ridiculous.

Social divisions are particularly visible here. Anne, who claims to have recognized herself in the character of *Girl, Interrupted*, comes from a very lower-class milieu. She is unemployed after gaining her vocational high school diploma, her father is a building painter, and her mother is a first aid instructor. Anne shows no reluctance identifying with mass cultural production. Conversely, Elsa, distinguished herself—the word "distinguished" is appropriate here—by a strong intellectualization and aestheticization of her practice. This is likely due to her family's valorization of purportedly legitimate culture. Elsa is a student in an elite Parisian university, her mother is a highly qualified secondary school teacher, and her father is a senior executive in the public sector. She regrets the increase of movies and reports on this topic. She wanted to be "the only one." Such reluctance to acknowledge the potentially influential role of the media in shaping an individual's self-harming trajectory is why I do not think that the interview method offers the opportunity to properly study the extent of media influence. Narratives about the media's influence depend mostly on self-presentation stakes, which are, themselves, subject to the participants' social-positioning issues.

However, from the moment they have been seen, read, or heard, these cultural productions systematically act on self-injury trajectories by providing a constellation of images related to the practice of self-injury, as well as depression, suicide, eating disorders, psychiatric institutions, and borderline disorders.

To what extent the media acts as an inspiration for individuals or as a reflection of a state of the population is a thorny question. Both cause and consequence of social activities, the media offers a certain legitimacy to the phenomena that it stages. Maya's narrative well illustrates this. She decided to tell her mother about her self-harming practices after watching a television show with her parents in which self-injurers were interviewed. Because they were addressed on television, self-injury issues acquired a more legitimate status, and thereby facilitated a conversation about it.

Of course, besides movies, series, and television programs, there is the internet. It can be hypothesized that from the 1990s, during which time the internet emerged and became massively widespread, a collective imagery arose around self-injury and the associated forms of malaise. In some blogs, the aestheticization of self-injury through graphic representations of blood, blades, death, childhood, and femininity is in vogue.

However, unlike the commonsense perspective, according to which self-injury would be, in some sense, transmitted through the internet, I noticed that participants often went to the internet to learn about self-injury after initiating this practice.

The internet represents less the opportunity for a transmission of the practice of self-injury than it does the dissemination of a coherent set of representations and symbols promoting its knowledge among the population, and especially its aestheticization and ritualization for those who have already started self-injuring. Although it is impossible to verify the specific impact these images have, we can certainly say that more people are aware of the practice of self-injury because of the internet's emergence and proliferation. As a result, self-injury has become possible for a growing part of the population. This has tended to gradually eliminate the prevalence of first injuries by innovation or importation, in favor of exclusivity of imitation.

The Spread of Self-Injury

The modes of entry into the self-harm trajectory are thus manifold: some *innovate*, others *import*, and most *imitate* either directly (through acquaintances) or indirectly (through the media or the internet). This typology allows us to understand how individuals come to self-injury.

It also helps us understand the spread of self-injury in the social world. Indeed, the distinctions between innovation, importation, and imitation suggest different forms of accessibility to this behavior. I assume that to come to a hitherto-unknown practice, the innovators had to be driven by particularly intense emotions. After all, they deliberately attacked their bodies without knowing why. Likewise with the importers, they had still considered their own death, which is undoubtedly an emotion characterized by a certain intensity. Conversely, the imitators seized a possibility already placed at their disposal. Most say that they would never have had the idea of self-injuring if they had not seen scars on others or been informed by friends about the effects of the wounds.

This hypothesis corroborates, in a sense, what some clinicians observe. Namely, that self-injurers would, over time, suffer less and less from severe "pathologies." Xavier Pommereau, a prominent French psychiatrist specializing in self-injury, has consequently differentiated what he calls a typical and an atypical form of self-injury.[13] While an atypical form would require immediate therapeutic attention and significant care, typical self-injury—even if it remains worrying—may be an almost normal response to the psychological stakes related to adolescence. From a sociological perspective, I interpret this analysis as a sign that fewer social conditions are involved in creating the idea and the urge to injure oneself. As this practice becomes imitable, individuals do not have to experience so intense a malaise to self-harm, as if they have invented the practice for themselves. In psychiatric terms, the idea of hurting oneself may come from less-severe pathologies.

The increased opportunities for imitative self-injury brought on by media exposure can be dated. Patricia and Peter Adler noted increased media coverage of self-injury in the United States, especially around 1996. A study of adolescent literature also noted the emergence of self-injuring characters in the 1990s, especially from 1991 onward. Finally, I showed in a previous work that French psychiatric literature on adolescent self-injury emerged in the mid-1990s and simultaneously became massively widespread in the United States (where the psychiatric literature first broached self-injury in the 1960s).[14]

The hypothesis of an increase in imitative self-injury from the 1990s resonates with the interviews. The second half of the 1990s represents a turning point. Most of the participants who had started injuring themselves in the 2000s were imitators, while most cases of innovation started before.

2 Toward a Feeling of Dependence

How does a vague and purposeless behavior, over the course of a few weeks or even in a few days, become a way of managing everyday life?

In the previous chapter, we saw that Annabelle described this transition with particular clarity: "A few days later I wanted to try again, and then a few days later, and then again, I realized that it made me feel good, so I continued." This is a classic case. Discovering the "beneficial" effects of the wounds makes people want to continue and maintain the behavior. For all the interviewees, this discovery is quite surprising, as it seems almost unimaginable, a priori, that such a practice would generate sensations perceived as positive.

However, for the participants, the relief triggered by the injury constitutes a temporary solution, or even the only solution in facing their daily malaise. Whether presented as the regulation of an internal suffering or of aggression, this relief is "worked out." Which is to say that individuals develop their practice, evolving their style of self-injury, as the frequency of injuries increases.

This chapter depicts the three processes underlying the evolution of self-injury with time: finding a method, ritualizing, and feeling the dependence. Distinguishing between the three is useful as different motives are at stake in each of them.

Finding a Method

The first mechanism consists in finding one's method of self-injury. It denotes the process whereby self-injurers orient the modalities of their practice so that it meets certain expectations as well as practical considerations.

The search for a method seeks first to attain the desired sensory experiences. It is an attempt to find a self-injury technique that bypasses undesirable emotions (such as anxiety) while arousing positive sensations (such as relief and/or satisfaction). For Mathieu, the attraction aroused in him by the scars makes his choice of burning quite obvious. Still, he tried to cut himself once: "I always burned myself. I tried cutting once and it did not appeal to me at all. I mean ... it's not much a matter of pleasure, but it didn't suit me. Well, it did not suit me. Me, I was mostly looking for scars, and I found that the cuts didn't make enough scars. So I immediately turned to burning" [face to face]. When describing failed attempts to find an appropriate method, participants often concluded with remarks such as, "it does not suit me," or "it's not a good match." Antoine said it as follows: "I had already tried to cut myself ... but only two or three times, it does not suit me as SI [Self-Injury]."

In parallel, self-injurers engage in protracted emotional work in order to better discern the sought-after sensation. This search materialized itself by the setting-up of habits, sometimes even a quest for the "best" possible habits, as depicted by Mathieu:

[Face to face]

INTERVIEWER: And you, basically, what was your ... [way of proceeding]?

MATHIEU: Me, I do it all the time in the same way, because, in fact... I ... how to say ... everything was oriented, everything was made to have a scar ... so from that point I ... I know there may have been better methods, but I used the method that was best for me to have the best possible burn, to have the best possible transplant, and then the best possible scar. So to have the best possible scar it was necessary to have the best instruments, to have the best heating material; finally it had to be ... it was a rather odd logic but ... how to say ... everything was oriented to have the best possible scar.

In addition to the search for sensations, finding a "good" method involves a search for discretion. Clémence, whose priority was that her self-injury remain inconspicuous, wondered about the places on her body where the scars would be the least visible. She alters her method as she changes her mind on this matter. Initially injuring her wrists, which she prefers in terms of sensation, she then moves to the thighs, and then finally to the feet. Annabelle aims more at increasing the intensity of her physical sensations. She describes three stages in the way she beats herself: initially she hits herself with her wrists, then she hits walls, and finally she strikes herself with objects. This evolution corresponds to her search for pain.

The successive changes in method reflect material and symbolic stages along the self-injury trajectory. Maya, who first stole her father's razor blades to cut herself, ended up using the "pretty blades" she buys in supermarket. She says she has "passed a gap" along with this change of object, a gap embodied by the incongruity of the purchase situation.

In this search for the best method, the participants follow a learning process similar to that outlined by Howard Becker.[1] Although this learning takes place mainly in a solitary setting, it is nonetheless a social process. Some discourses (such as the narratives of self-injury available online) serve to partly frame how one interprets the effects of the injury. For example, these narratives can provide terms and ideas that orient one's practice and aid its evolution. Mobilizing the collective imagery presented in the media is another way in which individuals might frame their actions. In particular, the symbolic approximation to death, which is desired by those who carry out their first wound as a step toward committing suicide, is a good example. This is because entry into the trajectory of self-harming can reflect dominant social representations of suicide, through the resemblance between suicide by incision of the veins (blood-letting) and self-injury by cuts. The learning process is also prestructured by primary socialization, both through previous experiences of violence and, more generally, through the development of one's relationship to the body.[2] In other words, the learning occurs alone, but the learner mobilizes resources acquired in the past.

The Ritualization

In some cases, self-injurers establish a set of habits, gestures, and stagings around their practice. That is, a "ritualization" takes place. Some participants speak explicitly of their self-injuring as a ritual, but beyond this, the term can be used to express the introduction of certain gestures independent of any material necessity into the self-injury method. These gestures can include preferences toward a specific context (place, time of the day, etc.) or some kind of special staging.

Elsa gives an almost ceremonial description of her self-injury. In her apartment living room, she listens to Mariah Carey's version of the song "Without You," cuts her wrists, and spreads blood on her face before watching herself crying in a mirror. Her self-injuring essentially becomes an artistic practice: "I found it beautiful, suffering, the mix of tears and blood." Elsa links her behavior with a broader aesthetic quest that she expresses, for example, in copying Charles Baudelaire's poem "The Destruction" on the walls of her room.

Conversely, Laomela, the author of an autobiography in which she narrates her self-injury trajectory,[3] refuses to listen to the music she likes when she hurts herself. For Laomela, self-injury relates to previously experienced sexual abuse, and to associate this with music that she likes would be inappropriate.

Continuing on what he seeks above all (the scar), Mathieu focuses on the objects to be used and the "maintenance" of the burn:

[Face to face]

INTERVIEWER: Was it also ... always in the same way?

MATHIEU: Oh yes, yes, yes, it was very ritualized ... I don't know how ... I think that generally speaking, according to what I read on the forum, people are generally attached to their tools, or to the way they do it.... They have quite specific ways of doing it.

INTERVIEWER: Okay. And you bought instruments especially for that or were they everyday things?

MATHIEU: No, when I first started doing this ... it was with a large meat fork, a butcher's fork, to heat on the gas, and when it was red, I applied it to the skin, and ... my roommate had confiscated my instrument ... and so, I was quite ... it pained me, eh? [*nervous laughter*]

INTERVIEWER: Yeah?

MATHIEU: Yeah, I was attached to the butcher fork because it worked well, it suited me well. So it bothered me when my roommate took it ... and so I was obliged to look for another instrument, and so I went to the DIY [Do-It-Yourself] row of the BHV [a big store in Paris] and found an instrument that suited me well, and so I burned myself with it from that moment. And so always ... always in the same way, I was heating on the gas, I applied on the skin, and when it was red at last, it was pretty gross actually.... It's always the same habit. Always, always the same. It's the same ritual all the time.

INTERVIEWER: So you integrated it into your habits ...

MATHIEU: Ah yes, yes, yes, and then I had always ... once I got burnt I was still very busy with my burns, I disinfected them, I took care of them ... there was the burn and then, afterward, there was all the ritual of care.

INTERVIEWER: What did you put on the burn? Are there special products?

MATHIEU: Yes, you have got to clean it properly.... Uh, when I had burned myself and I received a skin graft for the first time, I started to have septicemia. I was operated on in an emergency, because it has to be cleaned up quickly, because the wound was about to get infected ... so you have to clean it pretty quickly, so each time I burned a bit less to avoid infection, that kind of stuff. So it was necessary to disinfect properly, and then there was always this concern to have the best scar, well to maintain the sores so that it's ...

INTERVIEWER: But ... the less you take care of it, the more scars you get, no?

MATHIEU: Well, what I called maintenance was alcohol, irritants, it was more of that kind of stuff. I did everything to increase the sores; well, in short, they were not ... they were not very beautiful scars.

Usually, the ritualization is less intense. Arranging in advance the necessary tools for disinfection and privileging certain places of the body are the most commonly cited actions. This is the case of Maya:

[Face to face]

INTERVIEWER: And you were telling me ... well, we started talking about it ... that it was repetitive. Did you have any kind of rituals?

MAYA: Yes ... [*moment of hesitation*] let's say that after you ... [*hesitation*] eh, you already foresee what it requires thereafter to heal you [*hesitation*] ... so when it is at home, it is always in the same place in my room.

INTERVIEWER: Why a particular place?

MAYA: I was behind the door because in my room, I have no keys, and then otherwise in my high school, I had my favorite corridors, otherwise the toilets ...

The material setup remains minimal for most participants. However, this aspect may have been downplayed. Describing ritualization during the interviews caused much embarrassment. Since it risks placing self-injury into the social imagery of irrationality and madness, one can imagine—and understand—that some participants refrained from mentioning it.

Feeling the Dependence

All the people I met said that they quickly experienced a feeling of dependence on injuries; a coupled sensation of lack and need. Some even compared it to drug addiction. When Marie recounts her first burn, committed in the presence of a friend who cuts herself regularly, she talks about what followed: "In fact for her [her friend] it was like a drug and I realized that for me too now ... it's ... a drug ... and that's what ... when you cut your veins, afterward it's hard to do without. I know that even here [in the unit where she is hospitalized at the time of the interview], in the evening, I am on the verge of cutting myself" [face to face].

This sense of dependence gradually determines the frequency of injuries. The impression of a lack shapes a rhythm that develops over time, while the method becomes more and more definite.

The feeling of dependence also alters the initial motivation, which underlies the first wounds. Fabien is twenty years old and studying to be a specialized educator. He depicts very well the various stages of the self-injury trajectory:

> [Face to face]
>
> INTERVIEWER: It's curious, this moment when you restarted self-injury after your one-year break, I don't know, you said you "fancy" it ... what does this mean?
>
> FABIEN: Well it is ... in my opinion, there are several reasons why one can self-injure. There is the fact that one has things to express, like expressing ... it looks very scientific and stuff but anyway, to express an inner suffering in such a way that one can control.... And then there is the need, it's more, I would say more than ... when one self-injures by need, self-injury is closer to drug-taking, with a dependence, physical or psychological, I don't know, I never get the difference between the two; or, a pure longing, as someone might want to read a book or sleep with someone. And in my opinion, one arrives at the

stage of longing once one has tested one of the other reasons that can lead to self-injury and has exhausted this reason. For example, when you started because you needed it to express something, you do it regularly, and so on, and it turns into a need like a drug.... In my opinion it's more of a path.... One begins for a reason, then eventually needs it, and ends up wanting it. And the passage from needing to longing is rather particular though, because among the people I know, there are not many who have made the transition, and ... I mean, more theoretically, one can switch from longing to self-injury by boredom. At first, one wanted it, so the longing was drained as well, and finally one tries to fancy it again in doing it when one gets bored.

Expression. Need. Longing. Boredom. These phases keep coming back into the participants' narratives. Those who self-injure for the first time, as we saw, have a clear awareness of the circumstances (the present situation) and of the biographical moment (passage of their life) in which they find themselves. Self-injury therefore consists, initially, of an *expressive activity*: it occurs in a context that it expresses somewhat directly. The sensation discovered after the first injury—an immediate relief—enables the individual to temporarily attenuate the negative emotions associated with this context. Self-injury then becomes a *need*, because it appears to be the only (or at least the most effective) method of managing these negative emotions. It is at this point that the sensation of dependence occurs.

As the initial purpose of self-injuring fades and optimal methods of injury are discovered, some participants described the process of coming to derive pleasure from self-harm. The pleasure thus derived from the practice comes to supplant the impression of dependence. At this stage, knowing that others self-injure is significant, for it arouses a temptation. Some forum members say they struggled to manage their participation online as reading narratives of self-harm made them want to hurt themselves.

However, rarely did participants claim to have injured themselves when they were bored, or simply because they were bored. But boredom can figure as a kind of motive, especially when self-injury is so well integrated into daily life that it becomes a pastime like any other. This is what Maya says:

[Face to face]

MAYA: Sometimes, there is very weird stuff, so when you injure yourself all the time, several times a day, and so on ... and afterward you self-injure for anything. I think I may have hurt myself even for joy.

INTERVIEWER: For joy?

MAYA: Yeah. This is not something very common but I think I may have hurt myself even for joy in the same way I hurt myself because of boredom, when you're like, "Well, what can I do? Well ... Why not?"

3 Talking about Self-Injury?

SELF-INJURERS GENERALLY AIM to keep their practice secret. A survey completed among US students reveals that about one-third of self-injurers have never spoken to anyone about their self-injury. Only 4.6 percent reported it to a general practitioner and 21.4 percent to a mental health professional.[1] Most self-injurers say that they almost never talk about it with anyone, let alone with professionals, which other studies confirm.[2] My findings go in the same direction. Yet, where the participants live (Francophone Europe and Canada), many psychological services exist. It is easy to find a psychologist, a psychiatrist, or a doctor; there is no shortage of professionals to talk with.

How might we understand such reluctance to use these services? According to most professionals, adolescents and young adults experience difficulties in expressing themselves, accounting for their problems, and understanding the value of resorting to professional help. So, this reluctance is due not only to the suffering of self-injurers but also to the psychic specificities related to adolescence. In short, a pathological shyness supposedly dissuades adolescents from talking with adults who can listen to them. It is likely that, because of these perceived obstacles, various institutions and associations of health professionals regularly advocate building more listening facilities and setting up more links between the concerned professionals (psychologists, teachers, educators, social workers, and so forth). They reason that if young people are unable to express themselves, then it is necessary to build a network of qualified professionals around them, able to arouse their will to talk.

In my view, this reasoning is not exact. The people I met during my research speak very well, at least well enough to be understood. The few fears expressed about speaking of self-harm quickly dissipated during the conversations. The internet abounds with narratives. Young internet users are accustomed to writing about themselves. Moreover, self-injurers, like all those who experience any deviant practice, develop discourses of justification. In a certain sense then, these young people may be more able to speak than any others.

The reluctance to speak of one's self-injury behavior must therefore be framed differently, regarding questions of *to whom* they might speak, *to what ends*, and *with what risks?*

To whom? It is not because teens are reluctant to speak to a psychologist or a teacher that they have difficulty expressing themselves. If we wish to collect words, we must first ask ourselves to whom these words are said. Talking to parents, teachers, or friends does not imply the same stakes. This seemingly straightforward idea is apparently not that straightforward for most health professionals or health policies aimed at youth.

To what ends? Self-injurers do not all share the supposition that speaking helps. Reading the recommendations of therapists, one would be tempted to think that if every young person had a qualified adult to whom they could confide nearby, adolescent disorders would disappear. However, the relation between speaking about oneself and improving one's mental state makes sense only for certain social groups.

With what risks? Imagine telling one of your relatives that you are intentionally self-injuring. Just like you, the participants were afraid of being considered freaks. And they are probably right. A survey conducted on a representative sample of the French population shows that in response to the question, "According to you, someone who is violent toward himself is ... (Crazy, Mentally ill, Depressed, None of the above)," 22 percent of respondents opted for "Crazy," 42 percent for "Mentally ill," and 27 percent for "Depressed."[3] During my research, some participants told me that the discovery of their wounds by less-than-understanding classmates earned them reputations that are hard to bear: being the "crazy" of the class, a "freak," the "depressed guy," the "suicidal girl" of the high school, the "psychopath"—nothing terribly enticing.

And the multiplication of mental health structures does not change the risk of stigmatization, nor does it necessarily help with access. Self-injurers must know not only that mental health services exist but also where they exist. They must be aware that some psychiatric and psychological practices are free and that adult professionals will not make fun of self-injury; rather, they will treat it with a certain degree of seriousness and concern. Transportation and discreet access to facilities must also be ensured. Some participants would have liked to commence a psychological follow-up but withdrew their interest because of these issues.

This chapter addresses how self-injury is hidden or revealed by self-injurers to different interlocutors. It shows that this practice and the "mental disorders" supposedly associated with it shape the socialization of the people concerned, which disturbs the transition between primary and secondary socialization. Furthermore, revealing one's practice of self-injury can result in the intervention of agents of socialization (psychiatrists, members of internet forums, etc.) taking the place of friends through the traditional socialization process, such as at school. Consequently, even if self-injury may stop at a certain point in the self-injurers' lives, it nonetheless orients the very structure of their socialization.

Concealment Strategies

Whereas it seems much easier to remain silent than to talk, discretion is less the mark of timidity than a means of preserving one's relations in the social world. The participants put in place genuine concealment strategies, which I outline below.

- *Arranging one's appearance so as to cover the scars.* The participants often refrained from wearing short-sleeved clothing, even in summer, to cover scars on their wrists. Even with long sleeves, they acquire some gestural techniques intended to conceal the marks. Such techniques include avoiding raising sleeves or arms when presenting one's palm to an interlocutor. Wearing bracelets or long gloves may also be very useful.
- *Limiting one's participation in activities in which the scars may be visible.* Some participants say that they refuse to go to the doctor when they feel sick, lest their marks be discovered. Most of them find various pretexts and excuses not to go to the swimming pool, even when it is mandatory at school.
- *Preparing justifications if the scars are discovered.* In the case of cuts, deploying the so-called cat excuse is a classic technique, wherein one claims to have "a cat that often claws." In addition to the "cat excuse" comes the (less-plausible, in my opinion) barbed-wire excuse: "I fell in a field where there was barbed wire." In the case of burns, the pretext of a domestic accident suffices. Mathieu, to justify his regular absences at his work (his burns

required grafts and therefore prolonged stays at the hospital), has been creative. To avoid arousing the suspicion of his boss and colleagues, he claimed a genetic disease affected his skin, requiring frequent hospitalization.

- *Benefiting from others' experience.* Conversations between forum users and between hospital patients help refine these concealment strategies by exchanging "tips and tricks."

But despite all these efforts, somebody discovers the self-injury. This is because either the self-injurer decided to disclose it, or the scars are accidentally revealed. It is generally during "crises," such as suicide attempts, hospitalizations in psychiatric institutions, or ailments due to eating disorders, that family and friends become aware of the self-injurious behavior. These events suddenly make visible a practice that may have existed in the strictest confidentiality for months or even years.

Within the Family: Silence

The vast majority of people I have met say that there are serious communication issues in their families. Many express the feeling of not being able to talk about themselves and being confronted with ignorance, incomprehension, and even contempt from their relatives. In this context, concealment strategies stem from the impossibility of speaking while nurturing this impossibility. Such ambivalence likely explains why the participants remained dissatisfied, regardless of the family's reaction to discovering the self-injury.

The family members may notice the scars without any discussion taking place. In more extreme cases, a family tolerance to self-injuries arises, as it did for Louise. Without asking any questions, her father took her several times to the hospital when she needed stitches. Two hypotheses explain this silence. One can imagine that the discovery of a child's self-harm provokes the same risk of stigmatization for the parent as for the self-injurer, given the notion that teen disorders are caused by bad parenting. It is also likely that family members may be stupefied, simply not knowing what to do.

Another family reaction consists of setting up "psychological outsourcing." The relatives encourage or demand that their teenager consult a health professional. Elsa told me how her mother, after discovering her wounds, helped her make an appointment with a psychologist. The subject was not discussed anymore thereafter. If Elsa liked what she calls her mother's "respect for intimacy," the other participants whose parents only proposed they consult a professional have interpreted this reaction as a form of disinterest from their family. The story of Delphine, a twenty-one-year-old high school student in daycare hospital, is in this sense quite atypical. She began to hurt herself so that her mother would notice. She wished to signal her will to consult a psychologist after suffering sexual abuse, which she has had no opportunity to address. Remembering that this situation remains exceptional, Delphine's self-injury was a means to obtain psychological outsourcing. Most of the time, self-injurers complain about their family's apparent withdrawal of responsibility when they start a psychological follow-up. Instead of leading to a better consideration of their problems by their relatives, the follow-up seems to have the effect of unburdening them.

The third attitude adopted, the most socially accepted one, wherein the relatives attempt to chat to the self-injurers about their problems, fails to arouse enthusiasm among the participants. It should be noted that such a case is also very rare. Although this situation provides the self-injurer with the feeling of being heard, it appears to result only in outpourings of sadness, ultimately amounting to a form of psychological subcontracting. Annabelle, recounting this moment, concluded: "We have cried a lot and that's all." The few participants who have experienced this situation describe a circle of guilt. The parents show their good will and their guilt in failing to realize the difficulties facing their child, who, in turn, feels guilty for the problems that the practice raises, and so on.

The story of Eva, who associates her suffering with the sexual abuse she was subjected to by her former music teacher, is another exception. Her parents react in a way that seems to satisfy her. They support her in the legal procedures she has launched against her former aggressor and in obtaining membership to a victim association. Perhaps it is more satisfying *to do with* rather than *talk about*?

Some relatives establish full-fledged systems for monitoring bodily marks in a somewhat authoritarian way. At its most extreme this involves a formal prohibition to self-injure and the institution of daily controls of the self-injurer's body, a solution unsustainable over the long-term. These members of the family, once informed, do not take into account the behavior of the self-injurer, though they are aware of the actions, which paradoxically proves their unwillingness to confront it. It is assumed here that the strategy to be followed consists of monitoring what must be ignored, making sure not to see or say what must not be seen or said, and concealing what must be concealed. The strategy often requires hiding this practice from other members of the family, from neighbors, and more generally from circles of acquaintances. The self-injury of the child thus risks tarnishing the responsibility of the parents in the eyes of others.

The form of self-injury may change following the failure of concealment strategies. Some participants reported that they had to refine their method, for example, by changing the place on the body targeted for injuries. Others—and this is much rarer—even turn self-injury into a provocation to make their relatives feel guilty.

School Professionals

In middle school, high school, or university, the discovery of self-injury by staff members has different consequences depending on the formality of the framework, generating either an institutional follow-up or leading to an informal relationship. Note that many participants followed a normal education without their behavior being the subject of any intervention.

School nurses appear keen to anticipate the risk of suicide or other hazardous behaviors statistically associated with self-harming. As a result, they often opt for official guidance when they discover scars on their patients. This involves, among other things, informing parents, certain teachers, and health professionals (the school psychologist or an outside psychiatrist). Annabelle tried to commit suicide when she was in high school. Panicked, she went to see the school nurse who saw all the traces of self-injury on her arms and "reacted by calling my mother to tell her that it was her fault.... So, she wanted to warn all my teachers, the principal, and so on ... so at the beginning I said, 'Can I tell my parents?' ... It was because I didn't want to hurt them, she understood it like: 'they're going to react badly, they're mean, it's their fault.' ... I don't know, stuff like that. So she warned them" [face to face].

According to the interviews, this type of formal detection of the injuries largely disrupts the self-injurers' concealment strategies, while exposing them to a risk of stigmatization from their parents, their teachers and, if the news spreads, their classmates. Even if such disclosure leads to a desired psychological follow-up, most of the participants reported that they wanted to avoid it. From the moment that self-injury is formalized in this way, they no longer control how they are treated.

The narratives are more enthusiastic about relationships initiated in an informal mode. Some participants thus established relationships of confidence with one of their teachers, with close emotional ties being described as very strong and maintained even after they left school. According to the participants, this relationship of confidence offers, above all, the opportunity to address their issue with the addition of an adults' perspective, without necessarily warning any other actors. In this case, these teachers use relational skills more associated with their private rather than professional lives, which likely explains why some decided to end the relationship or warn other professionals against taking on a similar responsibility. Because they felt supported, the participants say that this type of relationship helped them sort out their issues.

Friendships, Conjugal Negotiations, and "Postcoital Downer"

Of course, friendly and affective relations are often a site of disclosure, given the confidence entailed therein. Here again, speaking of self-injury puts one's social image at risk. It is a bet: either the reaction is compassionate, indifferent, or negative. In the latter case, self-injurers risk a relational catastrophe. Such information may circulate very quickly, especially in schools. Not everybody is willing to risk potentially losing friends in this way.

Confidants and friends play a significant role in the evolution of the self-harming trajectory. Some become a source of inspiration. By their own practice, they encourage initiation of the first injury. Others, on the other hand, push their friends to quit the behavior. Some participants reported that they have made "contracts" with friends, committing them to stop self-harming. But these promises become obsolete as soon as a particular event makes the need for self-injury too strong or as soon as the friendship deteriorates.

More generally, one can notice that the practice undergoes a framing from the moment of the confidence. A friend's awareness, their fear and interrogation, and anticipation of their subsequent observation of potential wounds, does not systematically result in a reduction of self-harm. Around the self-injurer though, a form of discreet surveillance emerges, whose effect remains difficult to estimate.

Unlike when family members or school staff discover scars, the influence of the peer group rarely results in major breaks in self-harm.

Rather, the friends orient the daily pattern of self-injury. Acting in a fundamental role as advisors, they give meaning to these practices. The friend's intervention mainly takes the form of comforting the self-injurers, possibly helping them avoid certain wounds. This is because, as we will see, speaking to friends may constitute a possible substitute.

When they involve sexual relations, affective relationships make the scars visible to the partner (if the partner notices them, which is not always the case). More often than not, the response is supportive, but some participants report break-ups following the discovery of the scars or the admission of the practice. Annabelle recounts, with annoyance, one of her experiences: "Oh yes, there was one who dumped me after twenty-four hours, when he realized that. Then he told everyone I was completely crazy and that he did not want to stay with a girl like that" [face to face].

Entering a romantic relationship tends to favor a reduction in the frequency of self-injury, or even quitting, since de facto, this entails a regular checking of the body. It can also lead to a shift in the practice and reinforce concealment strategies. Clémence, for example, whose boyfriend cannot stand the idea that she self-injures while being in a relationship with him, transitioned from cutting herself on her arms to hurting her feet.

It is not only the frequency and the location of injuries that matter within the affective relationship, but their very meaning. From the moment someone enters a relationship, their self-injury involves not only themselves but also the relationship as a whole. The injuries may indeed be perceived by the partner as an offense, a challenge, or an attack on the viability of the relationship. Self-harming becomes part of conjugal life in the same way as disputes, infidelities, and disagreements, because it is often perceived as something done *against* the partner.

Élodie describes in striking terms another shift in the practice of self-injury under the influence of an affective relationship. She undoubtedly prefers burning, and had already tried to cut herself, or rather, to get cut by one of her sexual partners.

[Face to face]

INTERVIEWER: And so, you've never tried cutting?

ÉLODIE: Yeah, but never alone, because myself I can't do it, so I asked someone to do it. It has been a super enriching and intense experience, a bit difficult for the other person, but anyway ...

INTERVIEWER: It was not someone who self-injured?

ÉLODIE: [No], but a bit peculiar though. It was liberating because at the same time, it was also a privileged moment to do it with someone, but cutting myself ... I can't, I can't....

INTERVIEWER: And does it relieve you as much as the burn?

ÉLODIE: No. Because it was not ... the pain is absolutely not felt the same way. It is ... finally this type of pain I don't like it, it's something that doesn't suit me, that's not what I need.... Apparently they [people who cut themselves] are into blood while me, I'm really focused on pain.

INTERVIEWER: And did you do this several times, cutting with others?

ÉLODIE: No. I did it only once. I found only one person who agreed. I wanted to try at least once to cut myself.

INTERVIEWER: What kind of atmosphere was that?

ÉLODIE: There was something way more intimate and then a big downer, really super bad and ...

INTERVIEWER: Did he [her partner] feel bad too?

ÉLODIE: No, I don't think so. It made him a bit uncomfortable, because me, I was in a downer and I couldn't imagine burning myself in front of him and I needed it and that was the solution.... It seemed a good opportunity, at that time, to test cutting because we had precisely talked about it before, of the types of pain and all that. At the same time, it remained in the heat of the moment.

INTERVIEWER: Ah ... so it was not planned, was it just that you were feeling together in a downer?

ÉLODIE: That's it. Well we had ... because before we had discussed about how we self-injured and stuff.

INTERVIEWER: Was it something sexual?

ÉLODIE: Crazy, yeah. It was a moment of a ... what I call a "postcoital downer." I don't know, this is something we don't talk about much ... kind of when one has slept with someone ... there was a big peak of pleasure, and then suddenly, bam! Smashing down, big downer, panic attack, and so on. So, actually it happened in the frame of that relationship.

As we see in Élodie's narrative, sexual intercourse creates a social and physical connection that leads more easily to issuing atypical demands, in a depressing situation, or more generally. Shared bodily intimacy within a stable couple or occasional sexual intercourse, can lead to joint injury management. The eye of the other becomes, by anticipation, an integral part of the injuring process.

Internet Forums

Given the risks of stigmatization to which self-injurers are exposed over their social life, turning to the internet is a very understandable option. The possibility of exchanging anonymous experiences with other users sharing the same practice appears as a blessing. The taste for online conversations and integration into discussion forums does not reflect a supposed attraction of young people to new technologies. Rather, it is the effect of the intolerance of most social actors toward atypical behaviors.

The leitmotif of the studied French-speaking forums is "mutual aid" (*entraide*). Central to the presentation of these sites, this expression suggests that the forum makes an exchange of experiences around self-harming and related experiences possible. This exchange takes place both on the forums themselves and through more personal interfaces (private messages, instant messaging, phone calls, or face-to-face encounters). At certain points in the self-injury trajectory, this network of available interlocutors becomes a central circle of sociability. Being the only group where there is no fear of stigmatization, the forum is sometimes described as a refuge in the face of the outside world.

Integrating into online spaces requires a lot of time, as Clémence describes:

> [Face to face]
>
> CLÉMENCE: Well it's actually that I started to go on *MSN* [instant messaging software] because originally I didn't even know what it [self-injury] was. Because I had no account ... I had no unlimited internet account at the beginning, and after, as I was on the forum all the time, then you always propose, "yes, if it does not go ..." [implied: "come and talk to me on MSN"], and suddenly you say ... you feel a little bit guilty. You tell yourself that you will inevitably help them, you listen to them and everything, and you can't say, "Yes ... I have to go to bed ... I have school tomorrow...."
>
> INTERVIEWER: And so you spend your nights on it ....
>
> CLÉMENCE: Yeah. I spent nights ... I spent days ... frankly at some point it made me addicted to the internet. And when I woke

up … I woke up in the morning, I got connected, and then I went to bed at three or four am, and then I woke up a few hours later and I went back [on the internet] ….

INTERVIEWER: Was there always someone connected who wanted to talk?

CLÉMENCE: Yeah. There was always someone … and sometimes they are fine, and suddenly they're not … and then sometimes it was me that really needed it.

Online-built networks function as communities in which self-help is a value integrated into a gift economy. The exchange of experiences and the support shown within these exchanges are subjected to the same types of obligation in the gift/counter-gift systems described by Marcel Mauss.[4] Clémence clearly states that she is indebted for the support that one user gave her at certain moments. In other words, since her interlocutor read and responded to her posts and discussed her experiences, Clémence provided the same support; she believes it is a duty for her to be present when her interlocutors express the same need.

No physical obligation exists online, yet the moral system valued there—the system that maintains the reciprocity of the exchanges—goes so far as to compel one to eschew any perceivable constraints to being available online, such as going to school. In this context, mutual help is a skill. Forum users who are available and who give valuable advice enjoy a recognition that they generally do not experience offline.

Some would call these intensive connection practices an "internet addiction." But for participants, it is more a matter of adhering to an alternative social organization, based on codes of exchanges that value the reputation and relational skills of its members. For them, this differs to social life offline, which they perceived as more degrading.

What are the four main effects of participating in online forums?

1. *Making explicit one's history.* Writing on a website and talking about your issues requires being able to recount clearly the significant steps in your life and describe your emotions. Writing involves a work of self-expression and a description of the different developed practices. Because it occurs under the constant scrutiny of other members of the forum, this ability to write fosters the potential of internet users to find a way of telling their story, a way that is more socially accepted, and can be used outside the online forum context.

2. *An opportunity for comparison.* The process of socializing into forums allows self-injurers to compare their practices. These comparisons are carried out on two axes. The first concerns evaluating the severity of their practice. That is, they realize that their behavior is more serious than that of most participants, or vice versa. Knowing what the others do thus creates a kind of scale of severity. The second axis relates to the perception of self-injury. The members are led either to assert the "pathologization" of their behavior ("I realize that, like others, I have a legitimate problem"), or to minimize its severity ("because others do the same, I'm not crazy").

3. *A support network.* Frequenting internet forums creates a form of social support. The forum supplants the functions usually attributed to more traditional actors such as family, friends, spouse, support groups, or even patients' associations.[5] This online support network has significant advantages, including the availability of contacts who do not have to travel physically and are present at all times. Due to the time difference, the presence of users from Europe and Quebec makes a continuous turnover possible. Sometimes, this support function goes beyond online conversations. On one of the studied forums, members are invited to leave their phone number and address on the website, which allows moderators, for example, to warn emergency services if there is a risk of suicide.

4. *Provision of information.* There are many messages posted on forums that contain information about relationships with health-care professionals, care facilities, different methods to quit, ways to talk about self-harming with family members, and strategies for reacting to the discovery of scars in a school setting.

Health Professionals

Some of the people interviewed wanted to consult psychiatrists, psychologists, psychotherapists, psychoanalysts, and so on. Such consultations usually result in a marked improvement in mood, but are not described as essential to this improvement. In fact, in the consultation narratives, incomprehension prevails. Most of the time, the participants do not know what to think about the consultations. They do not understand the purpose of speaking so freely and struggle with not being told clearly what could "cure" them. The more determined ones made use of so-called shrink castings, attending appointments with many therapists to find the therapist that best corresponds to their expectations. Overall, professionals are most often seen as emotional supports, in much the same way as confidant teachers.

Let us note that these observations may depend on local contexts. For example, psychoanalytic therapies, which consist of very nondirective interviews, are widespread in Francophone Europe, and self-injurers may not feel the same incomprehension toward other forms of therapies, for example the behavioral approaches that are more common in North America. In addition, psychoanalysts are generally reluctant to prescribe medication, which changes the nature of the treatments—again, in contrast to North American therapists who are more willing to rely on drugs. Ultimately, social security systems play a role in the related trajectories, since even if private therapies are generally expensive in France, there is a whole set of free or almost-free public consultations, and associated medicine reimbursements. This makes possible the above-mentioned "shrink castings," even for those who do not have extensive financial resources. More generally, it is important to bear in mind that medical services are less expensive in France than in the United States.

Interactions with general practitioners, emergency physicians, or nurses may occur when an injury requires specific care, such as stitches, skin grafts, and so on. Such contact with the general medical system remains rare, and when it does occur, it is brief, although for some participants going to the hospital has become part of the routine of their practice. Some participants reported virulent misunderstandings on the part of health professionals working in the hospital context, and Amy Chandler's work suggests the same applies in the United Kingdom.[6] Participant narratives recount hostile reactions from emergency physicians who, in the eyes of the participant, sought to punish their patients by performing stiches without anesthesia. Louise recounts her experience:

> [Instant messaging]
>
> INTERVIEWER: Why without anesthesia?
>
> LOUISE: I assume (I mean I assume) that it was a form of "punishment" from doctors who (I quote a particularly stupid one) once told me, "I'm fed up handling teenagers in crisis that have fun slashing themselves" … in fact, it was never proposed to me, they may have thought that as I had inflicted the cuts by myself I would not need anesthesia. But, I know and I am sure that other

patients who came for accidental injuries were systematically entitled to anesthesia. Me, I was told, "it's useless."

INTERVIEWER: And how did they behave with you?

LOUISE: Quite brutal, not nice ... they were telling me off because I did not want to tell them "why," very indifferent otherwise. However the nurses and nursing aides were mostly very nice.

INTERVIEWER: Okay, it was the doctors who weren't understanding? After a while you did not know some of them better than others?

LOUISE: Yes, but they didn't react better, it was even worse when I saw some who recognized me. I was made to understand that I was wasting their time at the expense of "real patients who really need care."

The most striking example is that of Eva, who had a scalp wound stitched without anesthesia. Even if punishment is not intended, most professionals hold a strictly medical posture, often perceived as cold. They estimate the severity of the injury, usually benign from a clinical point of view; proceed to dispense the necessary physical care; and then eventually—but not always—direct the patient to a psychiatrist. These contacts with physical health professionals end up reinforcing the self-injurers' fear of being stigmatized.

Hospitalization in Psychiatry

Being hospitalized in a psychiatric institution produces a break in the self-harming trajectory. For the participants, there were two ways to enter an institution. The first way involves being directly admitted as a result of a suicide attempt or an instance of life-threatening behavior. Here, the initiative is taken either by emergency services, therapists, or by various germane actors. Caught off guard, family members, or school professionals will also often send the future patient to a hospital service. In the second case, which is far rarer, the hospitalization process takes place more slowly, when suicidal risk is not direct but "dormant," when the patient expresses and enunciates the possibility of voluntarily provoking their death in the short term, for example. Often, such enunciation will occur in the context of a preexisting relationship with a worker in the social or medical sector, from whom the patient is receiving support for another issue, such as anorexia or depression. In such cases, self-injury constitutes an aggravating factor in psychiatric institutionalization, usually discovered afterward by hospital staff members.

Professionals tend to perceive self-injuries as indicators of suffering. They take note of this to acknowledge the "psychological suffering" of their patients, but afterward, only pay the injuries themselves secondary attention. The professionals observed during my internships in psychiatric facilities no longer remember exactly which of their patients self-injured. Nonetheless, they maintain interest in elements considered to be more important, such as the family situation (in particular the personality of the parents) or the trauma experienced by the patient.

Hospitalization significantly alters the relationships between the patients and their family and friends who, at this stage, are likely to learn of their self-injury practices and possible involvement in other deviant behaviors. This is often a time of profound revelation for the family. In the school environment, if the news of a student's hospitalization spreads, more than ever the student faces the risk of being stigmatized as "crazy." This label is very difficult to escape from, even when other people display their goodwill. Lucille, a sixteen-year-old high school student, told me that her classmates learned about her hospitalization. One of her teachers, in an attempt to avoid a rough return to school for Lucille, prepared a special welcome, a snack with a banner that read, "Welcome back Lucille." This put her in an even more uncomfortable situation.

Hospitalization also changes the practice of self-injury itself. In mental health institutions, unlike general hospitals, some empathy is maintained toward self-injurers. Obviously, the behavior is discouraged, or even formally prohibited by means of a (sometimes written) contract with the assigned psychiatrist. But the feeling of dependence, which I have addressed above, threatens the viability of such a commitment. When the patients feel that they can no longer restrain themselves from self-injuring they find more discreet methods, using different objects, since as a preventive measure, cutting objects are prohibited in psychiatric hospitals. For example, the use of razor blades is only permitted under the supervision of a nurse. The intense circulation of information between patients also facilitates changes in the self-injury practice. In such institutional environments one learns very quickly of many self-harming techniques that were previously unimaginable. Finally, as patients notice that injuries are likely to be detected by caregivers, they change the meaning given to self-harm. In part, the practice loses its intimate dimension. It is then embedded into the care relation, where it figures either as a means of arousing the recognition of one's suffering, or as a provocation.

By generating a change in the practice, hospitalization can make self-injury a symbol of self-control that the institution cannot thwart. What Maya says on this matter is insightful:

[Face to face]

INTERVIEWER: So, you did not try anything other than cutting?

MAYA: Uh, if I told you [*laughs*], I also hit myself and, what else was I doing... oh, yes, I was scratching, but that was especially when I was in hospital that I developed all these things. That I hit myself especially ... so ... because, of course, we have nothing to cut ourselves ...

INTERVIEWER: Ah, yes, there are no blades ...

MAYA: Exactly! So I hit myself until I fell to the ground. It was the same, it became a ritual, it was really ... [*silence*]

INTERVIEWER: What was the ritual in beating yourself?

MAYA: Well, I struck myself, every time one heard "boom," they [the nurses] ran up, I couldn't stand up anymore, they carried me ... they made me go out to walk, and so on. So, every time it was the same thing ... I hit myself and waited for them to arrive, I was bored of hitting myself. And like that, I started scratching myself there.

INTERVIEWER: Okay, still because there was no actual ...

MAYA: Yes.

[*Silence.*]

MAYA: And burning also, I forgot.

INTERVIEWER: Did you try it too?

MAYA: Bah, I was burning there too.

INTERVIEWER: In hospital?

MAYA: After leaving I continued some stuff, you see.

INTERVIEWER: Oh, okay. You continued what, after leaving?

MAYA: Well, I just kept going. But ... for example, the blows, a lot less. Because it makes noise and ... outside the hospital where I wanted people to react, sometimes ... but I wanted to be helped, it's true that I wanted to be helped, but I didn't know what to do about it. But ... outside I may have hit myself once or twice, but otherwise ... I kept burning myself, scratching myself.

INTERVIEWER: But how did you burn? Because at the hospital, it must be protected enough, this kind of stuff, right?

MAYA: Actually, everyone had lighters, because everyone smoked except me, and ... so I had a lighter, I didn't smoke, they could have taken it away from me, it's funny they let me keep mine, and ... I had a lighter just to hurt me. And ... I was heating hair clips, and burning myself with the heated clips. But you know, actually, if you want to hurt yourself you will always find the way to do it, because, they said to me, "but what are we going to do, Maya, we'll have to take all your hair clips." But after that I would have heated anything else in metal, I don't know, a fork, I don't know, something around ... I had asked a girl who wrote to me [in a forum] ... Laetitia, so Laetitia was hospitalized too ... and she wrote me a letter one day, telling me that she could always hurt herself, that she hurt herself in the shower; actually, she put hot water to the max and she hurt herself like that. So you see it's really ... it's something I've never done, but ... but when you want to hurt yourself, you always find a way. It's ... I often thought about it, no one can ever stop you from harming yourself, even if you are tied up you can still I don't know, bite your tongue. You see when you're hurting yourself that's ... [*change in intonation, indicating importance*] you have control over yourself, and no one can ever take this control away.

* * *

From the moment someone carries the marks of a socially illegitimate behavior, they can justify themselves either purposely, by confiding in relatives or pursuing a psychological follow-up, or under constraint, after the discovery of the marks.

Thus, self-injurers must take into consideration a set of external parameters: Who will see the scars? Who knows? What consequences may self-injury have? This is one of the deeply collective aspects of self-injury. Individual and intimate at first, this behavior entails a form of quasi-strategic anticipation work. In the family, at school, within friendship circles, at work, on internet forums, in conjugal relationships, or in a hospital, what to do if the scars are seen? Depending on each configuration, self-injurers have to adjust the meaning and the practical modalities of their injuries, often torn between the will to confide and to maintain secrecy, all the while struggling to keep control over the potential means of disclosure.

Here, it is worth highlighting the numerous attempts, in the psychological literature, to characterize what self-injury is once and for all. Whether it is to be understood as a help-seeking behavior, an attention-seeking one, or a secretive one, makes little sense regarding the ambivalence of self-injurers' trajectories. I would more accurately assert, in line with Peter Steggals,[7] that the possibility of self-injury is embedded within the contemporary collective belief that feelings must be expressed lest a malaise emerge—hence, the metaphor of the pressure cooker. Furthermore, as Amy Chandler explains,[8] self-injurers are stuck between morally connoted poles, from the positive help-seeking to the negative attention-seeking, which complicates the issue of disclosure.

Let us finally notice that talking about one's practice does not necessarily involve giving up this practice on a regular basis. Indeed, whatever the help sought, the confidences made, or the people informed, it remains possible to self-injure daily without anybody noticing.

4 Quitting

MANY PARTICIPANTS HAD stopped (or almost stopped) self-injuring at the time of our interviews. How did they do it? How did they succeed? The reader will be disappointed in anticipating some definitive explanation or clarification on this matter. The reasons for quitting self-injury are even more vague than those for beginning. Generally, though, two forms of explanation are mentioned.

First, practical constraints can reduce one's interest in self-injuring. For instance, when immediate family and friends seem to suffer too much from the practice, self-injurers end up blaming themselves. Similarly, in the context of a new activity or workplace scenario the risk of one's self-injury being discovered can become too restrictive to continue the practice. And second, the emotional state of self-injurers may improve enough such that the dependence on self-injury fades.

At the junction of these two explanations—one "practical" and the other "emotional"—three elements appear to play a leading role in quitting self-injury: psychological follow-ups, the impact of relatives, and the feeling of "clicking."

Psychological Follow-Ups

Consulting a mental health professional is a commonly cited factor in quitting self-harm. Participants often discussed these consultations when seeking to interpret the improvement of their condition after the fact. They understood the positive effects of therapeutic consultations, offering assertions during the interviews such as, "Looking backward, I think that my shrink helped me a lot." Given that therapy is often undertaken over a long period, and we have nothing other than these after-the-fact descriptions from participants, we cannot definitively demonstrate the effects they describe. In the intertwining of between words, actions, and thoughts, we cannot identify the impact of psychological follow-ups on the trajectories of the participants. It is simply impossible to isolate what follows from therapies and other life events.

However, we can consider the interesting relationship between the facts (the therapy itself) and their representation (what is said about it thereafter). First, the very decision to consult a professional indicates the individual's impetus toward ceasing self-harm. In other words, those who are seeking professional help and consultation are already those who wish to cease self-injuring. Second, putting confidence in the potential outcomes of psychological follow-up matters as much as the content of the consultations. According to professionals themselves, desire on the part of patients to convince themselves of their own "healing" is one of the necessary prerequisites to an effective therapeutic experience. I assume that the performative effect of therapies, as socially legitimate rituals initiating the cessation of deviant activities, sometimes accompanied by equally socially legitimate drugs, fosters quitting.

It is striking to note that the participants judged their therapist in two ways. When they consider that the therapy is well suited to their needs, the therapist is described as a support, a confidant, a nice and pleasant person to whom one may speak sincerely. In other words, the therapist can become a professional friend, and, in this case, the participants sometimes feel overwhelmed by what they have discovered of themselves during the sessions. As Samuel Lézé notes regarding psychoanalysis, analysands associate their follow-up with the personality of the therapist, who comes to physically embody the representation that patients construct of their therapy.[1] This charismatic personality may become a providential figure who has rendered possible a turning point, a break, a change. But when the therapy does not work, the therapist is then evaluated according to professional criteria: "This shrink was incompetent."

A final point must be emphasized. Therapy, as a socially legitimate "cure," also legitimizes in retrospect the deviant behavior that it has helped stop. The same process can be seen in the case of young offenders who, when supported by socio-educational structures, develop a discourse of recovery, reformulating their past misdeeds as "youthful errors," which they have managed to overcome.[2] In the same way, the passage through therapy enables the participants, when they talk to a sociologist, to present their deviant activities (self-injury) as having been overcome. They have learned to dissociate with words their previous actions from what they are now.

Relationships

It would be tempting to assume the importance of the support offered by one's network of acquaintances in the move toward quitting self-injury. As is often the case, the issue is more complex than it seems. It should first be noted that the word "support" encompasses a wide variety of acts. For instance, we support someone who self-injures when we take care not to stigmatize their practice, that is, by not telling them that they are crazy, for example. We support someone when we agree to spend time talking with them about the issues underlying this practice. We are supportive when we suggest leads for interpreting these issues and when we provide concrete advice to assist them in getting better. Indeed, we also support self-injurers when we are materially accommodating (in accommodating them when something goes wrong), or by simply being present, physically or online, during difficult times.

Through the interviews, my impression is that specific support activities mattered less to participants who stopped injuring themselves than the possibility of them engaging with a supportive person. The feeling of being surrounded by people who can potentially offer some support is more important than the support itself.

In our second interview, Constance, a twenty-six-year-old social worker, reports that settling in a shared house with other members of a forum and socializing with a regular circle of friends has greatly reduced the frequency and intensity of her anxiety attacks. The support provided through her new living circumstances and friendships has proven sufficiently effective such that she has almost stopped self-injuring:

[Face to face]

Honestly, already, I feel less anxious. Basically, there are way less situations that cause me anxiety, already, I think.... Honestly, I'm pretty scared of loneliness and abandonment, and there, on this forum, I found quite a lot of people who are solid around me, friendships that are solid, that stay the course. So already, it's less a page on which to feel bad and to get anxious. Even more so since we see each other regularly, and even more since I have two roommates who are from the forum. Yes, honestly it's going to be better on that side. And when I get anxious, I admit that ... I mean I have the impression that before there were so many little things on top of each other that made me so anxious that any small thing could make anxiety no longer bearable.... I was constantly anxious, and the smallest thing happening was too much. While now, it takes a lot of layers before I arrive at a point when I say, "Oh fuck, there it really must stop." I mean a bit of anguish, we manage to bear it, it's bearable, it's not too overwhelming. So, honestly, it's true that I have not found many alternatives, so that when the anxiety really becomes too unbearable [I don't self-injure] ... but as there are fewer things that make me anxious, it is way rarer that anxiety comes to a point where I say to myself, "Well ... there ... scissors."

This is representative of statements made by many other participants. We do not exactly find a desire for specific care, but a desire for a solid social bond; in other words, a desire for a *possible* support.

We must also emphasize the importance of support specifically dedicated to the practice of self-harm. Such support includes a friend to talk to, a teacher to help analyze underlying reasons, and so on. This type of support seems to produce a double effect. First, the relationships associated with this support are retrospectively formulated as a determinant factor in quitting. "Hopefully she/he was here," I have often been told. Many interviewees reported repeated conversations with a friend or confidant teacher who helped them get better, or else helped them understand what they were experiencing. Second, these relationships have the paradoxical feature of decreasing in intensity should self-injury cease. Put simply, the support provided subjectively enhances the desire to get better, to discontinue self-injury. But feeling better potentially generates fewer instances of this support and can consequently lead to a possible recrudescence of the malaise associated with self-harm.

Such a mechanism can be observed directly online. This is because, in specialized forums, self-injury initially justifies and undergirds the link between people. Camille explains the resulting tension:

[Face to face]

INTERVIEWER: What effect do you think participating in forums had on you?

CAMILLE: Uh ... paradoxical. On one hand it really incited me to do more damage, deeper [injury] because I saw that there were people doing it and so, that I dared more to do things, they didn't necessarily give me the idea but ... yes; actually, I don't know. On the one hand, when I started on the forum it became a lot worse and on the other, actually, being in a community that pushed me to stop, it really helped me stop. Actually, to be "cool" on this forum, you must want to stop. So, to be in the … I mean to get comments and attention you had to want to stop, so it's true that I was sixteen and drawing some attention was very cool. And it's true that to draw attention I began to quit.… It's still a means of getting support, I mean we all know each other quite well, we all create friendships, links, and there is still, yes, if you say that you feel bad you'll still have support and not only just your buddy. For example, yesterday a girl sent me a PM [private message], she wrote: "Fuck, Isa, she's not doing well at all, I'm afraid for her, she doesn't want to answer the phone, can you call her parents?" There are things like that, after that I call her, we chat. So, let's say that it's more than words on a screen. And especially, now that we do a lot of ERL [Encounters in Real Life]! So we know each other quite well in real life too, and it's true that to stop self-injury can also be seen as a loss of support, the feeling of no longer having its place. So it's paradoxical.

For this reason, the valorization of quitting self-injury and the opportunity for members who quit to remain a part of the community is a significant stake for the moderators of the forums. The forum users who want to stop self-harming thus maintain the possibility of keeping their circle of sociability when they finally succeed in quitting. This configuration is the same for friendships created during hospitalizations. Losing one's connection with the psychiatric context jeopardizes these relationships because their foundation must then be redefined.

Finally, I would like to suggest another possible explanation for quitting self-injury relating to the self-injurer's social network. Stigmatizing reactions or negative judgments expressed by friends or relatives (through mockery, breaks of contact, etc.) on learning that one is self-harming do not seem to be taken into consideration by those who recount how they quit self-injury. No one will tell you—indeed, no one told me—that, "it helped me a lot that people made fun of me and called me a freak." However, we can imagine that stigmatization may contribute to weakening the legitimacy of self-injury in the eyes of self-injurers. Therefore, stigmatization might play an indirect role in fostering the discontinuation of self-harm.

The Rhetoric of the "Click"

Guillaume, a twenty-four-year-old German language student, stopped injuring himself two months before receiving his high school diploma.

He said that he "clicked," and suddenly felt disgusted by the cuts he was inflicting on himself. Catherine, a twenty-two-year-old psychology student, provides a similar explanation:

[Face to face]

INTERVIEWER: You stopped eating disorders through self-injury, and then what made you stop self-injuring?

CATHERINE: Well, I don't really know. Given that I didn't want to continue doing it every time there was a problem, I don't know. Gradually I reduced and then I don't know, one day I stopped.

Guillaume and Catherine did not have any clear motivation to quit at the specific moment they did. However, their narratives tell us about a widespread feeling. Namely, the awareness that self-injury is not a definitive solution to their problems; it is only temporary. However, there is no reason for this behavior to remain only temporary. It is quite conceivable that an individual would continue to self-injure until old age. The question is, why does the pathological, deviant, and inappropriate representation of self-injury become significant enough to trigger, at a certain point, the rejection of this practice, when for years it only provoked the desire to conceal its discovery?

From a practical point of view, the efforts undertook to conceal bodily marks—which become increasingly elaborate as the self-injury trajectory progresses—come to seem progressively more irrational to the participants. For Mathieu, the daily the situation became far too restrictive. His burns required skin grafts, requiring major hospitalizations, work disruptions, and excuses to relatives, friends, and his employer. At its most extreme, this led him to invent a genetic disease to justify his absences. But how long would it have been possible to credibly maintain this pretext? These constraints provoked him to stop burning himself (even if he started again after our last interview). Others are afraid to find a job where the scars would be visible and then become sources of discredit. These participants described how such measures ultimately limited their future possibilities. Finally, when relatives learn about self-injury, their increasing involvement in the daily management of the practice—supporting or controlling it—may give the participants the feeling of being a burden, which decreases the appeal of self-harming in their eyes.

The rhetoric of "clicking" must also be analyzed in relation to age-related issues. Self-injury is often understood as distinctly adolescent behavior. This representation is supported by a statistical reality (presented in the introduction of this book): self-injury mainly involves teenagers. The prevailing idea in the existing literature is thus that it is the state of being adolescent that incites people to self-injure.

But we can reverse this idea and interrogate what effect this social labeling has on the practice itself. Because it is conceived as an adolescent or juvenile behavior, self-injury can appear more easily conceivable during this biographical period, and inadequate afterward. Participants such as Guillaume or Catherine therefore feel that they will stop doing it at a certain point, that they will not "keep doing it all their lives." Soon, they will no longer be within the socially accepted age bracket that can feasibly resort to this kind of behavior. Like Danny Glover, who incessantly repeats in *Lethal Weapon 2* that he is "too old for this shit," quitting self-injury after "clicking" may mean that, for some self-injurers, a change has occurred in their age-related positioning. As adolescence ends, so too do the behaviors associated with it.

Can We Quit?

It is commonplace to associate quitting self-injury with "getting better." However, this is not always the case. On the one hand, some stop harming themselves because of others' incitements. On the other hand, some resort to substitution behaviors, such as eating disorders (anorexia and bulimia). This engenders a concern—shared by some moderators of most internet forums—that encouraging cessation may, in fact, also encourage the replacement of self-injury with even more physically damaging behaviors. These replacements include intensive alcohol and drug use, suicide attempts, eating disorders, and so on. Do these substitutions then really constitute a stop? Of course, voluntary injuries cease, in the sense I have defined them, but self-aggression may not.

Furthermore, while the end of the self-injury trajectory does imply the end of the regular recourse to injury, it does not imply the cessation of irregular, periodic harming. All participants claiming to have stopped self-injuring also reported having done so periodically in the years following cessation. These relapses—this is what they themselves call them—occur in response to events perceived as particularly destabilizing and painful. This is distinct from their earlier, regular, self-injuring that was precipitated by no significant trigger. All the narratives suggest that the self-aggressive reflex, once acted on, persists in a "latent" form.

For example, Camille succeeded in reducing the frequency of her injuries, but was suspicious of the idea of quitting (just as above, she was suspicious of the idea of beginning):

[Face to face]

I had, let's say ... stopped.... Finally, I never ... there was no moment when I was like, [*dry tone*] "I quit" ... I mean ... it's ... there was a time when I actually said to myself, "Come on, twice a week, I can't even walk because my legs are full of injuries, I can't take it anymore." So, I stopped like that, but I never ... I mean there are quite a few people when they stop they absolutely want to have their normal way of life back. "I am healed, clicking, I will explain everything to you!" I've never claimed to be cured, I'm not cured ... I mean ... yes, basically, I still have the impulse to react stupidly ... it's true that when there is someone who tells me something stupid, that hurts or irritates me, instead of yelling at him ... well, I'll punch a wall.

Examples abound; surely participants quit self-injuring, but only as a mode of daily emotional management. The "impulse," as Camille says, remains. The disposition to react to disturbing interactions through self-aggression is difficult to stifle.

5   Self-Injury on a Regular Basis

WHAT IS A typical day when you self-injure? We must first understand that self-injury is not a unit of action. It takes place through several steps, each of which involves different motives and emotions. This is what Anne recounts in our first interview:

> [Face to face]
>
> INTERVIEWER: And about what you feel, what does it do to you actually? Um … in general, before you cut yourself, do you feel anxious for example?
>
> ANNE: No, I am not anxious because I'm about to do it.
>
> INTERVIEWER: Okay, so … it's really positive?
>
> ANNE: Oh yeah, telling myself that I will do it, I know I'm gonna do it, and I say to myself, "Anne, you're really stupid." There are several phases in a cut, you have the phase where you're going to do it, then you do it, and … during the act you feel something, and after, you have the phase after the cut when you get … it's hard to say … I mean, hard to understand … but you're like getting your kicks … and me, what I do is that I close my eyes … [*Closing her eyes and mimicking satisfaction*] and I hold my arm like that, and I fully feel what I have done.

In this chapter, we will follow self-injury as a process, a succession of steps whereby someone is led to self-injure and then experiences its after-effects. While Patricia and Peter Adler, or Amy Chandler put emphasis on the various ways of doing and feeling self-injury, my theoretical aim here is to elucidate a generic, common process. This is less an attempt to contest their claims, than it is to trace an adjacent line of inquiry.

The process of self-injury in question lasts a few minutes, a few hours, or even a few days, and has an important property: at any time the individual can interrupt it, or go back to the previous step.

Triggering Events

The process usually starts with a disturbing situation. You do not know how to interpret something a friend may have said. Perhaps an argument breaks out between your parents. Maybe someone in the street stares at you disturbingly. Or a bad grade provokes disappointment. These disturbing situations are not especially unusual, but they certainly create a feeling of misunderstanding, uncertainty, or injustice. When I ask Benoît, a sixteen-year-old high school pupil, to give me an example of what kind of situation prompts him to self-injure, he recounts what happened on his birthday:

[Face to face]

BENOÎT: That day I had gone to class ... I went back home, I went down to the kitchen to set the table, wash the dishes.... They [his parents and two brothers] come, they put their feet under the table, I don't talk during the meal ... during family meals I never speak. My father tells stories, you've heard them forty times before, always the same, so it annoys me. And then comes the moment of the cake, I clear the table to set the plates for the cake, I take out the cake ... "Go do the dishes!" They eat the whole cake, I do the dishes. I come back to the table; no one's left ... I eat my cake in a hurry. What a nice birthday! The gifts this year were the worst. I got a pen and a toolbox to repair bikes and to repair stuff in my room. On my brother's birthday the month before, he got an Xbox [a game console], so ... if you like ... it made me a little upset.

INTERVIEWER: So ... afterward, you went up to your room?

BENOÎT: Yes, I was angry and then I locked myself away ... [*silence*]

Such triggers, evidenced in Benoît's account, typically produce what Erving Goffman calls "embarrassment,"[1] which describes the way a participant in a given interaction does not know how to behave anymore. The participant then seeks to conceal the expressive signs of this embarrassment (agitation, facial redness, etc.) because these signs can expose the individual to social stigmatization. I chose this notion in order to conceptualize the situations associated with the trigger event because it includes almost every identified triggering possibility. Indeed, whether it is an argument with a friend, the death of a relative, or a sudden obsession for self-harming, the common point remains the inability to behave as usual.

An important characteristic to note about such embarrassment is that its triggering does not provoke any visible reaction from the others. It is likely that Benoît's parents failed to notice anything, simply observing their son going to his room. Trigger events are embarrassing situations with no physical or verbal reaction from the embarrassed person.

It is an absence that can be explained by the inability to find any solution to resolve the problem or by the fear of how persons who have prompted this embarrassment might react. For example, Benoît says that he prefers not to disclose his discomfort, as he fears facing hurtful remarks or indifference, which would aggravate his feeling of injustice in a family where the expression of emotions is uncommon.

The more individuals move along their self-injury trajectory, the more they control the relief that the injury provides. In turn, this increases the likelihood of banal events triggering the process. Louise illustrates this well, stating that: "It can be about dumb stuff. For example, my neighbor who borrows my hair dryer without telling me, or I ask her something and she forgets to do it. Things like that."

For some people, self-injury becomes so integrated into daily life that a trigger is no longer needed to start the process. When this occurs, we can recognize the shift from "expressive" self-injury to self-injury by "need," "longing," and "boredom." As time goes by, the trigger disappears from the process. Alternatively, the trigger may even be deliberately set up. Some participants explain that they have forced themselves to think about painful topics or have deliberately placed themselves in uncomfortable situations in order to inculcate themselves the urge to self-injure.

Of course, though embarrassment triggers the self-injury process, it does not explain it. Many other parameters are involved. Nonetheless, the trigger of the first injury seems particularly meaningful for the participants. These situations often remind the participants of the subjectively negative aspects of their trajectory. Benoît's feelings about the evening of his birthday refer less to the evening than they do to the very devalued role that he feels he holds in his family. Another recurrent example involves participants pressured by their families to succeed socially. For the participants, a bad mark at school or the pejorative remarks of a teacher are frequent triggers.

The Autonomization of Thoughts

The day continues. But the triggering event has initiated some unease. The individual's mind focuses, wanders, extrapolates, rehashes. The situation, now passed, persists mentally. What Charles Cooley calls "inner conversations"[2] seem to gradually *autonomize* from the situation in which they originate. By *autonomization* of thoughts, I refer to a kind of inner conversation that follows an embarrassing interaction, but the topic of which is no longer the embarrassing interaction itself. Indeed, starting with the embarrassment related to a particular situation, the individual's thoughts are consumed by anguish, seemingly without reason, without finality, expressed in a form of intense mental wandering. The participants often describe this as a "panic attack." Physical signs accompany the panic attack, such as tremors, nausea, and unusual bodily sensations. Sometimes the trigger is linked to past events through an association of ideas.

These narratives, which seem to be a matter of introspection, "psyche," or psychology, are first and foremost product of culture. The participants describe a "feeling of emptiness," the impression of being a "bummer," "self-hatred," the impression of "exploding," or "going nuts." In short, they recount experiencing a form of pure suffering, with no other object or recipient other than oneself. This indicates a typically Western or Euro-American emotional framing, according to Catherine Lutz. Lutz contends that the ability to feel an emotion independently of a context does not exist in all human societies, and is even specific to Western society.[3]

This autonomization of thoughts momentarily reconfigures the subjectively negative aspects of the self-injurer's trajectory. For example, though Anne says that she does not regularly think about how she felt when her father decided to sever ties with her, she focuses on this severing in her moments of anguish—themselves linked to other triggers—and experiences a similar feeling of abandonment. Eva explains that, in these moments, she may physically feel the presence of her former sexual abuser, now deceased, whereas the triggering event might just have been that she broke a plate or that her mother did not like her clothes. Benoît explains: "Often, I think of something and all the other stuff comes back into my mind. There is my father who speaks badly to me, for example, before he leaves the house, and [when I am alone,] I think about what [my parents] said to me the day before, and about my schoolwork, and about everything" [face to face]. The autonomization of thoughts also results in a form of loneliness. This solitude has a material and mental dimension. With regard to the former, the distraught individual seeks physical isolation, as Benoît did when locking himself in his room. Regarding the latter (mental dimension), participants described disengaging from interactions, their minds drawn elsewhere.

Withdrawal, in either the material or mental sense, does not entail emancipation from social constraints. Other individuals and forces may still be able to direct social control over the self-injurer. Indeed, in situations of loneliness, individuals can no longer expect their acquaintances to produce feedback on their "face," in Goffman's sense of the word. Goffman specifically studied how people, during interactions, try to "keep face" and try to ensure that the others behave with them in such a way that they feel that their social status is acknowledged. In Goffman's words, "keeping face" relates to "the positive social value a person effectively claims for himself or herself by the line others assume he or she has taken during a particular contact."[4] Isolating oneself, materially or mentally, entails one's removal from such involvement constraints (glances, gestures, or words). In such a situation, self-injurers are left alone with their thoughts.

"Anxiety," the word regularly used by participants to describe the autonomization of thoughts phase, ultimately denotes an inability to keep face for oneself. This explains why many start self-injuring when the balance between solitary moments and moments spent with others becomes unstable. Indeed, numerous beginnings or relapses occur when isolation increases (e.g., due to holidays, or strikes) or, on the other hand, when moments alone become scarce (as during school trips, or any period of nonstop community life). Note that this balance between solitary and non-solitary time functions as a social standard of well-being. The historians Georges Duby and Philippe Ariès have shown how recent the inception of this norm has been in the West. In their eyes, the need to spend moments alone emerged in the eleventh century in the West.[5]

Dismissing the *Equivalences*

During the autonomization of thoughts, self-injurers feel disempowered. Haunted by negative emotions, unpleasant thoughts, or having the impression that they do not know how to think anymore, self-injurers can no longer fully perform their social roles. Under these circumstances, high school students cannot keep up with their lessons and workers are unable to do their jobs successfully. Furthermore, the emotional and physical effects of the autonomization of thoughts are difficult to bear. Individuals then seek an escape. Self-injury thus appears as an option, as Marion Deville-Cavellin explains in an autobiographical account: "Each crisis of panic ended in a bleeding, practiced with stoicism. A few razor shots so as to separate the skin into two abrupt cliffs of flesh revealing a vermillion torrent, and the shining wound prevented my mind from flying too far."[6]

But injuring oneself is not the only way. There are other behaviors that can put an end to the autonomization of thoughts. That is, other behaviors exist that can initiate a form of "emotional work"[7] sufficiently effective to escape from it. To a certain extent, these behaviors are interchangeable with self-harm, insofar as they produce a similar effect. I call these behaviors *equivalences*. Anne gives an example: "Generally, when I cry, I do not injure myself. But it has already happened that I cry and I self-injure at the same time, it was at a time when it [the feeling] was so strong that I couldn't evacuate [the suffering] otherwise" [face to face]. For Anne, self-injury and crying produce the same type of effect, but with different efficiencies. When she feels anxious, she uses the easiest and most effective practice to alleviate this emotion. Self-injury then intervenes either directly or as a reinforcement of another ineffective practice, such as crying.

Some equivalences are very common. These include talking to a friend, crying, playing sports, writing, or eating. For the first of these examples, we can imagine the importance of the internet, and especially instant messaging, in facilitating lines of communication with friends. Contacts are constantly available and regularly connected, thanks to networks formed through the forums. Other examples of equivalences include alcohol or recreational drug use (though these are very uncommon), listening to music, watching movies, playing video games, and taking anxiolytics. Some commitments increase the attractiveness of equivalences, such as informal promises to friends to stop hurting oneself, or more formal constraints, such as a workplace where a scar would be too easily visible. More generally, the social stigmatization of self-injury, internalized by the participants in a moral register (they say that it is "wrong" to harm themselves, "one must not do it") also encourages the search for equivalences.

The use of equivalences to overcome anxiety requires prior knowledge of or experiences with these equivalences. Some psychiatrists advocate learning such behaviors to encourage their patients to stop harming themselves. Thus Barent W. Walsh speaks of "replacement skills."[8]

This raises the question of the individual receptivity to this or that behavior. Why are some effective and others not? Why do some spontaneously come to mind and others do not? From childhood, emotional conditioning frames our expressive resources. Take the example of crying. Several studies have investigated the management of crying in newborns and shown that we are prepared, from our early childhood, and depending on our social environment, to adjust our emotional expressions in difficult situations.[9] Since birth, crying is channeled by people around us; we *learn* the situations in which it is appropriate to cry or not. Primary socialization also shapes our behavior toward food, our relationship to language, the maintenance of friendly networks, dispositions to write, and so on. Thus, the equivalences—crying, eating, writing, talking to a friend, and so on—are drawn from a set of skills partly learned from childhood. The potential equivalences available to self-injurers are therefore inexorably tied to the various processes of socialization, commencing from birth.

Furthermore, the acquisition of equivalences proceeds through what is called secondary socialization. This learning may take place during therapies (for instance, a therapist teaches their patient other ways to calm down) or even within ordinary conversations where participants talk about the tips and tricks they use to cope with stress. Internet forums act as reservoirs of equivalences, especially through posted narratives from which forum users draw inspiration.

[Excerpt from a forum]

I had only one idea in mind, banging my head against a wall, but I controlled it, I controlled myself, I have a certain control now.... So I decided to put into practice what I have often heard for a while, I mean doing intense physical exercise, because it secretes the same stuff in the brain (I've forgotten the exact word) as self-injury does, or about the same. I used to do a lot of sports before, martial arts, soccer, and sometimes I used to play hockey in the street, etc. Now, I have neither the will nor financial means anymore. Anyway, all of that is to say that that night, I spent an hour in intensive karate practice, I was hot, this did me so much good, yet it took me another good hour after to sleep, even if I was completely exhausted. I wouldn't say it gives as much satisfaction as self-injury, but it made me feel good.

One might wonder then, why the participants continue to self-injure, having identified equivalences to their self-injury. Throughout the process of self-injury, three concrete reasons explain this.

First, these equivalences require some material configuration to be put into practice, at the precise moment of the autonomization of thoughts. In this regard, self-injury remains a very accessible behavior, because it is easy to hurt oneself in any place with any object, unlike many equivalences. It may be difficult to cry in public, for example, or to play a sport at a given moment, to talk to friends in the middle of the night, to eat when one cannot gain access to food, and so forth.

Second, the autonomization of thoughts renders the individual unable to perform certain actions. Talking to a friend or watching a movie requires one to stay minimally focused. However, injuring oneself may be performed at any degree of self-control or anxiety. Physically and mentally, it is very simple. For instance, Louise, who has made a habit of speaking with friends to stop self-harming, had a relapse on a day when she felt too "locked up" to talk:

[Face to face]

LOUISE: I can't really say what triggers it [self-injury], outbursts of rage actually, when I feel irritable, even when someone talks to me.... So, there, this is what happened this summer, the simple fact that someone had talked to me, I actually experienced it like an aggression, and I really needed to calm that rage down, to let it out in one way or another ...

INTERVIEWER: Usually, do you have other means to....?

LOUISE: Usually I try to talk, but that day I couldn't, I was locked up and it really was as though I were imprisoned.

Third, self-injury is for self-injurers the most effective way to alleviate anxiety. While they can stop self-harming and find alternatives to their behavior, nothing seems to equal the relief brought about by the act of inflicting a wound. It is for this reason that some participants occasionally use an equivalence and then, when this equivalence does not have the expected result, turn ultimately to self-injury.

Preparation

Depending on the type of wound intended, self-harming requires minimal preparation. Indeed, if it is possible to self-injure in any material setting—you can, after all, hurt yourself with your own nails—some features can improve the efficiency of the practice. The features include finding a sharp or a burning object nearby, seeking a location to inflict the wound, or preparing disinfectant in advance. The duration of this preparation phase varies depending on the envisioned material devices and the actual situation.

Mental preparation is also required. For example, some participants say that they spend the day imagining their next injury (thinking about the place on the body, the object used, the location of the act itself, the moment, etc.). Doing so already provides a degree of relief, as it enables them to direct their thoughts. Others anticipate the interactions that may result from the injury, as Eva describes:

[Face to face]

> When I got to emergency to be stitched up, it's true that I often did that ... but I noticed early on, it should happen when there's a psychiatric nurse there. Because there were five [psychiatric nurses] and I got along very well with them, and it's true I often ensured I cut myself when they were here, to speak with them. I wouldn't succeed in ... for example, when I felt bad, what they told me is to go to see them before cutting myself, but I said to myself ... as if it wouldn't be legitimate, as if ... hmm ... if I didn't cut myself they wouldn't take care of me.

What is particularly interesting to note in this phase of the process is the hope expressed by some of the participants that someone might discover their preparation and encourage them to give up the behavior. Some interviewees told me that they might go to a supermarket to buy new razor blades, hoping that cashiers would prevent them from self-injuring. Of course, this never happens, which is why I qualify these pleas for help as *virtual*. We might assume that such absence of reaction elicits some bitterness, which may in turn reinforce the autonomization of thoughts. Louise relates this yearning for outside intervention:

[Face to face]

INTERVIEW: Under what circumstances did you self-injure?

LOUISE: I felt very bad; I was on medication that wasn't suitable at all. I blamed my shrink for it, because it had been months since I told him that my treatment wasn't suitable anymore. He was on holiday; I had the impression that he had completely scrapped me.... I was really, completely in distress ... and I needed to do something to calm it down. So I went to buy razor blades and ... it really was a cry for help, all I wanted was for somebody to prevent me from buying them, and at the pharmacy, when I bought stuff to take care of me [disinfectant], I wanted someone to ask me to stop ... nobody did that. So I cut myself again.

Because it involves visible objects and practices, material preparation constitutes the last bulwark before the wound. This is the final point prior to self-injury at which the intentions of the individual have a small chance of being discovered by someone, resulting in an interaction that constitutes an equivalence. It is at this point, when no equivalence has been forthcoming, that most self-injurers give up hope of abandoning their preparations.

As the self-injury trajectory progresses, the preparation phase of the process is carried out more and more rapidly because the necessary material elements are prepared in advance. Over time, creating routines makes it easier to take action. Placing razor blades in a pencil case or a receptacle, a cutter under the bed, a lighter in the glove box, enables the act of self-injury to occur with relative convenience and ease.

When preparation is complete, the wound can be made.

After the Injury

But the process does not end with the act of self-injuring. The pain caused by the injury persists. This prolongation of the effects differs depending on the chosen mode of injury. People who cut themselves, except in extreme cases requiring stitches, feel the pain of scarring for a few minutes, hours, or (more rarely) days. Most participants explained that they waited for the pain of the injury to subside before re-injuring. Thus, individuals who cut recommence faster than those who opt for burning.

After injury, the scar can then be "taken care of." Some prefer not to treat the wound. Some disinfect thoroughly. Others try to aggravate their wounds, either by applying irritant products or by self-injuring again in the same place, to increase the pain and/or enlarge the scar.

Finally, the coexistence of fearing exposure and the desire to have people discover the scars, reveals the ambivalence toward the visibility of self-injury. Eva describes such ambivalence: "It was little calls for help, hoping that people would see it, and it's not possible because I found so many excuses that ... well no, it's really not possible. And I've always been like that, trying to issue small clues but never doing it all the way" [face to face].

Self-Injury Process: An Example

The steps presented above outline a typical pattern of the daily self-injury process. But these steps may be of variable duration and, above all, they do not succeed one another mechanically. The narratives published on internet forums eloquently depict the form this process takes, since they retrace all the states through which the forum users have passed in the immediate aftermath of the event of self-harm. Due to the smaller duration between wounding and retelling, narratives published on internet forums are, arguably, more accurate than interviews. In the following text, Mélusine, a sixteen-year-old forum member, fully shows the tangled nature of the stages: "Sorry for coming here.... But I need to calm down.... Things go wrong! Things go wrong, things go wrong, things go wrong.... I don't know what to do ... I can't go on like this ... I can't stop going round in circles, I feel like I'm going to crack up! ... I MUST NOT!!"

The author of these lines initially portrays the impression of losing emotional control. This sounds like an autonomization of thoughts, which leads to a difficult search for equivalences. Mélusine "goes round in circles," and is afraid she will "crack up." No equivalence appears available at the time, which fosters the idea that only a self-injury would properly obviate her anxiety. Moral reluctance is the last line of defense: "I MUST NOT!!" Mélusine then looks back on the genesis of her emotional state:

> Today was a really shitty day. Today I really had a shitty day.... Last night and this morning, everything was ok.... I partied with friends, and it's true that I had the blues, a bit, but everything was still OK, I was in control. I smiled, and it wasn't hypocritical. I "slept" at a friend's house, then I came back home.... I sat down at my computer, I spoke, I searched for things.... In short, it went well. A friend whom I really care about phoned to see me. We had a date. This guy is lovely. I don't tell him about my life, but he takes so much care of me.

In Mélusine's account, she was not initially facing any difficulty beyond a slight feeling of sadness. There was no potential trigger: "It went well." Moreover, her smile is qualified as sincere.

> So I smile again for the day, but to be in good form I sleep a little. I wake up at the time of the date, but as I feared, I'm feeling a bit down. He calls me.... I tell him that I haven't left home yet.... He's sore at me.... It's normal.... I say to him "No, don't worry, I'll be there in twenty minutes," but no ... my ex-boyfriend, whom I still love, gives me a call and

I don't know if it's because I'm tired or something but what he says has more impact than usual. I don't feel at all well.... I cry. He cries. We cry. I don't manage to stop crying. He keeps me on the phone because he knows that I'll go to see another guy.... He's feeling very bad and me, too kind, too fucking stupid, I support him, I help him and it all gets even worse.... After an hour I end up hanging up on him and I go out to join the one who's been waiting for me for an hour and a half now.

At this stage, Mélusine does not feel "very well," as she feared. Her romances put her in an embarrassing situation, in the sense that she does not know how to behave anymore. This inability is reinforced as her emotional state prevents her from full self-control. A potential trigger emerges. Potential, because we do not yet know what will occur after that. The young forum user could progressively feel better, but this was not to be the case:

And there ... I break down.... My tears begin to flow and don't stop. They gnaw at me so much because they are full of pain. I can't stand it anymore. I think of the guy waiting for me, and I say to myself: "No, you can't go like this, calm down first." So I call a friend.... She doesn't answer the phone. I try again and again. In the end she picks up.... She doesn't manage to calm me down. I hang up. I go around in circles, I pace. I can't stand it anymore. I can't handle it. Now it's five o'clock and this nice guy finally texts me, saying he doesn't want to see me anymore, he doesn't like to be taken for a fool, that I have to call him if I want to stay friends, otherwise "it's over." I can't blame him, he's right ... but ... from 5:00 to 7:00 p.m., I find it impossible to calm down.... I cry. I have panic attacks in the street, alone on my little street.... There are a few passersby and they look at me as if I'm mad.... And me, I'm just waiting until this finishes.

Here, Mélusine enters into what I have called the autonomization of thoughts. She "breaks down" and finds herself unable to fulfill her social roles. "You can't go like this," she says to herself. Seeking equivalences, she cries and speaks to her friend, neither of which provide the necessary alleviation. In this situation, using an equivalence turned out to be impossible. After receiving a text message from the "nice guy" with whom she had a date, her anxiety worsens. She notes the inappropriateness of her behavior, which she opposes to the qualities of the young man:

After a while, I look down at the ground and I spot a piece of glass. Images flash before my eyes.... I think of hurting myself. NO! I

MUST NOT DO IT!! I text my ex, to avoid screwing up. While he's the one who hurt me so much, he's also the only one who knows how to calm me down ... how to prevent me from screwing up when I feel like that. I didn't want to but, even worse, I didn't want to hurt myself for this. NO AND NO!! He succeeds. I calm down and go back home. I smile at my parents ... we go out to eat, near a bar where I often go.

Stirred up by the sight of the piece of glass, and hesitating to self-injure, Mélusine tries to find another equivalence that would allow her to calm down. Here we can notice, in Mélusine's writings, the systematic association between feeling bad and self-injuring. This association tells us about a certain advancement in the self-harm trajectory. In parallel, she keeps face, writing again about her smile (now a hypocritical one) that she displays to people she interacts with.

Everything goes well, I nearly calm down until I see a guy who I had a messy break-up with. I act like I don't see him but then, shit, I'm not running away from my problems. But no, I can't move. A crisis starts again ... I tell my parents that I'm cold.... They believe me but they are chatting with some friends and so we can't leave. So, I go to see this friend and we begin to talk when a mutual friend, completely drunk, begins to pour out everything and anything, very loudly.... I'm feeling worse and worse. The same images flash in my head again. No! NO!! NO!!

While the process that might lead to self-injury seems to stop, a new event disturbs the fragile equilibrium that Mélusine has just found. She faces a new potential trigger—seeing this embarrassing ex-boyfriend again—and the autonomization of thoughts. She notes "a crisis starts again," stating "I can't move." But the material impossibility of searching for equivalences, given that she is in a restaurant with her parents, and the accumulation of embarrassing events drive her straight to the perceived need to self-cut: "The same images flash in my head again."

And then we go back home, I've told my mother that no, nothing's upset me because I don't want her to feel uncomfortable, but I'll receive a lot of remarks.... I don't wanna see them [these friends] for a while.... I don't wanna see anyone. I wanna hurt myself.... But I must not. I keep myself busy. I keep myself busy. And I keep myself busy. It will pass. I know I won't crack. But I'm afraid though ... but it calms me down a little, to write all this and it makes me cry. However stupid it may seem, the need passes. Now I regret having thought about it.

While she expresses increasing difficulties "not to do it," Mélusine comes back home, where she can begin to search for equivalences again. This is because the different material configuration enables the search to begin anew. She tries diverse activities. Then, she writes this message that we have just read. She cries as well; this time successfully, since her desire to self-injure has faded away.

In summary, self-injury is less a type of action as such than a *disposition* to action. It is a *liminal state* composed of several steps that do not necessarily and mechanically lead to an injury.

6   On the Ways to Self-Injure

THE ACT OF self-harming provokes a transition. With a single gesture, self-injurers effect not a reversal of their situation but an emotional turnaround. In doing so, they seek a sensation with the aid of another. Taking Hochschild's concept,[1] this emotional work is realized through a binary emotional system (the emotion to be discarded, the emotion sought), which grounds the subjective logic of the act.

For some, the desire to feel pain is paramount. Others insist on witnessing their blood flow. Sometimes the attraction for scars prevails. Multiple patterns exist. How to explain these variations? In this chapter, I argue that different social trajectories lead to different social experiences. These differences in trajectories and the resultant experiences contribute to the formation of different symbolisms, which shape certain sensibilities to certain objects, feelings, and practices. To address this question, I will focus on the smallest scale of analysis—the act itself—drawing on my interviews with Marie, Fanny, Cécilia, and Élianor, four young women I met during their hospitalization in a closed psychiatric facility.

The Clean and the Dirty

Marie is fourteen years old, and is completing her eighth-grade studies. I met her during her third hospitalization in the psychiatric unit for suicidal adolescents. Her most recent hospitalization followed an attempted suicide by drug overdose. An accumulation of events seems to have precipitated her taking such action, including an appointment in court and an argument with her ex-boyfriend. Her medical file indicates that her two first admissions to the hospital also resulted from attempted suicides. Marie's suicide attempts are accompanied by an increase in self-injury by cuts and burns, which her file mentions occur "in a context of school dropout, nocturnal awakenings with anxieties, increasing violence at middle school and intensive use of cannabis."

According to Marie, her family situation is marked by the divorce of her parents eight years ago, and by her parents' personalities. Her father regularly says that he is ill and that he suffers from very serious syndromes like Charcot's disease (which, according to doctors, is not true). Moreover, he seems to have been violent during Marie's childhood. Marie describes her mother as someone "sad," "not authoritative enough," and who took antidepressants following her divorce. Marie tells me that she does not forgive her mother for failing to protect her from her father when she was little. She currently lives with her mother and two sisters.

According to Marie, two particular events triggered her feeling of unease in the year before our interview. They coincide with the beginning of her self-injury. The first one was intoxication with GHB (a psychotropic causing a state of disinhibition and memory loss, nicknamed the "rape drug"). Marie accepted some at a party and woke up the next day, hospitalized, and without memory of the evening. The second event was her performing fellatio on her ex-boyfriend, without physical constraint, but while feeling obliged. She was afraid that he would kick her out in the middle of the night. She is marked by that evening. A psychologist she was consulting convinced her that the event could be considered a rape, a label that reinforces her unease.

In this delicate context, Marie says she feels lost and involves herself in a series of deviant activities, such as violence against herself and others. Unlike most of the interviewees, her practices are both self- and hetero-aggressive. She emphasizes their expressive dimension, especially in regard to suicide attempts: "I just wanted to get noticed, it was not to die." She recounts several assaults that she committed on classmates or other patients, recalling insults aimed at nurses or teachers. According to her, the target of her violence depended on the situation. "At school, as soon as someone upsets me, I fight and that's it." At home, by contrast, she favors aggression on herself, "because with my mother, I can't fight . . . and when I cry so much that I have emptied all the tears out of my body, and that I still feel bad, that's the only solution."

Her first self-injury happened one day as she continually cried, in the presence of a friend who advised her to burn herself with a cigarette. Surprised, she realized that this practice "relieves" and repeats burning herself. A few months later, she "goes over to" cuts, while gradually managing to control her outbursts of violence toward others. The cuts seem "cleaner," "less disgusting." She also prefers to see the blood flowing, as for her, it represents an "evacuation." There is, therefore, a channeling of aggression into self-aggression through cuts, an evolution presented by Marie as a quest for cleanliness.

Marie's narrative intertwines her sexuality, self-injury, and more generally, her feeling of unease through the lexical field of cleanliness. Since her "rape," she says she finds herself "fat," feels "dirty," and sees herself "as a bitch." Concerning her lifestyle, she suffers from bulimia crises, sometimes making herself vomit when she feels "too dirty" and, at the same time, becomes a "cleanliness maniac," obsessed with household order and neatness. She says that she behaves voluntarily "like a whore," inviting young men to her home and having sex with them, among other things to get free cannabis.

Marie classes her behavior and bodily sensations as either clean or dirty. The social identity that she stages and narrates is divided between these two symbolic poles. Rape, intensive eating, the feeling of being fat, the consumption of cannabis, problematic sexual encounters with men are presented as dirty, hence the violent qualifiers that she uses to describe herself: "slut" and "whore." But her obsession with cleanliness, voluntary vomiting, and self-injury are associated with clean behavior, since they act as means for restoring a symbolic cleanliness. The most obvious example of this search for cleanliness is her transition from burns to cuts, where cutting represents the evacuation of what she sees as dirty in her.

From Violence to Violence

Fanny is sixteen years old. She recounts a rather hectic story. She grew up on the outskirts of Paris, in an atmosphere where she constantly either witnessed physical violence between other family members or suffered it directly from her mother, who is casually employed as a domestic helper. Her life has been marked by the suicide of her father, who worked as a mason. One day, as she came back home after a party, she discovered him dead, his throat cut, lying in a pool of his own blood. At that time, she lived with her mother, her sister, and her brother. Soon after, her mother met a man on the internet and spent a few days at his home in the south of France. After a week, her mother decided to settle in with him and moved the whole family there. This man, however, suffered from terminal cancer. Family life began to revolve around his disease, his daily care, and accommodations his care necessitated. Fanny recounts that she closed herself up at that moment, and that she stopped talking to anyone and started self-cutting. Tempted to break objects and feeling powerless before the observation that "it was useless to talk anymore," Fanny self-injured out of anger.

Surprisingly, our conversation took place in a very relaxed atmosphere. We laugh a lot. Despite what her injuries evoke, Fanny speaks of them with a degree of satisfaction and humor. She describes the pleasure she feels in hurting herself, while being aware that this solution is only momentary: "The issues, they don't disappear like that, but it's [self-injuring] still pleasing though." The young woman explains that she "fights evil with evil" and asserts that seeing her scars "makes her smile," because they remind her of what she has done.

Our conversation ends strangely. When Fanny seems to get tired, becoming less coherent in what she recounts, I thank her, tell her that the interview is over and turn off the Dictaphone. But she stays seated and begins to enumerate an impressive list of ways she hurts herself, among which are some more indirect self-injury techniques such as pretending to fall down during sports classes. She boasts about the size of her scratches and valorizes the set of deviant behaviors that she was inspired to perform.

Regarding self-injury, her goal is clear. She wishes, above all, to experience pain. The practical modalities of her injuries illustrate this, for they reveal that she is engaged in a process of optimizing pain. For this, she gradually switches from cuts to burns. While for Marie, the wounds were destined to reestablish an emotional order oscillating between the clean and the dirty, Fanny channels her anger to cope with the uselessness of communication. She sets up her self-injury, over and over, as a reproduction of her violent environment. She wants to express the anger that accompanies her personal story every day, and which she struggles to express due to her family's move to the sick man's house. While Marie had made the transition to cutting to develop her symbolism of cleanliness, Fanny, does not share such concerns. Fanny wants to feel pain, and any way of proceeding is good, as evidenced by the multiplication and progression of her self-injury methods.

For Fanny, the exaltation of violence consists in repeating the same pattern. Communication seems useless to her, which makes her angry, which in turn, leads to the injuries. Finally, everyday domestic violence engenders routine self-inflicted violence, through a sort of adaptation mechanism to a situation lived as a dead end. Fanny's emotional order, characterized by the anger/violence dialectic, thus somehow strikes a balance; a balance that is no doubt precarious but nonetheless succeeds in making daily life more livable. A last detail, anecdotal but revealing: Fanny has recently stopped burning herself. She has been dissuaded from continuing by her new boyfriend who threatened to hit her if she starts again.

In Search of "Normal" Bodily Sensations

Cécilia is a seventeen-year-old, twelfth-grade student, studying in a science track that offers mathematics, ancient Greek, and music options. Such an arrangement constitutes one of the most distinctive settings in the French high school system. Her parents divorced when she was thirteen. She offers a very cold image of her father, a cardiologist, whom she describes as demanding and materialistic, manifesting his emotions only through gift giving. Cécilia says that she gets along better with her mother, who is a nurse. She finds her "cooler" and "more attentive." She has two brothers: a fourteen-year-old who lives with her father, and a nineteen-year-old who studies computer sciences and lives alone.

Cécilia's history is marked by various manifestations of anguish. As a result of a water skiing accident, she began to suffer an increase in panic attacks; she uses the word "spasmophilia." She was afraid of dying: "I realized I was not immortal." More generally, she experiences strange bodily sensations that make her uncomfortable and make it difficult for her to feel as if she is in her own body. While these disturbances used to arise only in the morning—and Cécilia used to be able to manage them by taking "some time to integrate [her] body"—they now last several hours and break out at any time, especially when she is alone.

Cécilia dates her problems back to the divorce of her parents. At that moment, regular arguments between her father and mother provoked panic attacks. But it was mainly the suicide of her aunt, to whom she felt very close, which marked her: "I really felt like passing into another reality. When my mother told me she was dead … it was not possible, there was a problem of adjustment, and it was as if we had passed into another dimension." When her parents divorced, Cécilia experienced a similar sense of unreality, albeit to a lesser extent: "That too, I thought it was not reality."

At the same time, she talks about her feelings of guilt. Before her parent's divorce, Cécilia explains having imagined, "what would it be like to have separated parents?" Similarly, before the death of her aunt, she said that she had thought that "if someone close to her died, [she] would recover her emotions." Having imagined these events before they occurred sometimes leads her to think that she shares responsibility.

She explains that after her aunt committed suicide, she needed to "feel something" in order to cope with the sensation of "unreality." She hit a wall "until there is blood" but, not experiencing any relief, she took a cigarette to burn herself. The anticipated effect occurred, and she began to "return to reality." Discovering the effectiveness of self-injury, she decided to start again as soon as the disturbing sensations return. She explains that she went "a little further" (in terms of physical intensity of the wounds) during each of the four burns she inflicted on herself. "It's always in the same context.... I'm not feeling things anymore and I need to shake myself," she said, evoking "either a panic attack or moments of emptiness, total emptiness."

What is striking about Cécilia's story is the strangeness of her bodily sensations and the difficulty she experiences in describing them. "There are moments when there is no more touch or anything, it's rather frightening." She expresses a very negative image of her body: "I thought I was full of shit, I was having a hard time breathing." An abundance of obscene words pepper the conversation. When I point out to her the violence of her remarks, the teenager answers directly: "Oh, I know, but it's really the impression I have, of being a rot."

Cécilia reports that she made the conscious choice of burning herself rather than cutting for two reasons. First, the burn produces more pain, and this sharp pain is necessary to help her regain bodily sensations. Second, this method "lasts longer," meaning that the wound inflicted by burning continues to cause pain longer than that produced by cutting. However, the momentary relief triggered by the burns diminishes with repetition. She therefore plans to stop burning.

Here, the purpose of self-injury is to either terminate bodily sensations perceived as agonizing, or to recover bodily sensations themselves. It is no longer a matter of evacuation or of anger, but the search for a sensation of reality, for the intelligibility of lived experience. In this case, the physical, and by extension, emotional shock, produced by the wound prevails: one must "get back down to earth," quickly.

Self-Inflicted Justice

Élianor, a fifteen-year-old student studying in the ninth grade, was hospitalized after a suicide attempt. She spoke spontaneously at the beginning of the interview: "It was when I had too much hatred toward myself, but it wasn't especially anger toward people ... it was by accumulating hatred toward myself, errors.... Me, before, it was like, I was making a mistake, it was a cut."

Her high expectations relate to her family: "I'm very close to my family.... If I disappoint my brother and my sisters or my parents, it hurts me, so I cut myself." In fact, our whole conversation revolved around this idea: her parents, her ten-year-old brother, and her two sisters of eight and five years old, are what is most important to her: "What affects me the most, my weak point, is my family. If they are hurt, it hurts me, and when it's me who hurts them ... well, I punish myself." Of course, this attention reflects a good relationship: "My parents, they are super nice with me."

Élianor's father works as a gardener. Her mother, after completing a degree in architecture, decided to give up the potential career that this degree opened to her to become a stay-at-home mother and thus devote more time to her children. Élianor emphasizes the alternative character and personality traits of each family member, which distinguishes the family from the others. She describes her family through clothing and personality traits that are rather caricatural: her father, inspired by hard-rock bands of the 1980s, collects manga figurines; her mother, "completely Buddhist" dresses "in all colors"; Élianor boasts a Gothic style and is inspired by mangas.

This feeling of difference permeates her relations with her peers. She says that she is sidelined. Physically assaulted several times by young people from her school, she interprets this situation as a consequence of her nonconformism. She has been insulted "because of [her] style," for her so-called Aryan race because she is blonde, or as a "dirty Gothic whore." These aggressions affect her relationship to her body. Élianor has repeatedly dyed her hair, partly in response to insults targeting it, and regularly cuts it due to a particularly violent attack in which she suffered a wound to the scalp. She also has begun a diet so intense that it provokes fainting.

She began to self-injure in 2008, and stopped three weeks before our interview in March 2010. The first time was in reaction to a breakup. "Suddenly everything has risen to the surface," "everything" referring to the aggressions she suffered. She then kept self-injuring, but for another reason: to punish herself. Élianor insists that feels self-hatred when she commits a "mistake." "I wanted to be almost perfect, I mean, as best I could, so I wigged out and I cut myself.... The only thing I found was cutting or burning."

Of course, one wonders about the mistakes that lead Élianor to punish herself. Ultimately, they are insignificant, which Élianor knows: "These are the mistakes that every teenager makes, but I can't stand them, it's like my parents say, 'don't do that,' and I do it." For example, she spoke of a time when her parents did not want her to keep her cell phone at night. One evening, she kept her phone anyway, and made some calls. This resulted in her exceeding her monthly plan of fifty euros. She reimbursed this amount with her savings, and was reprimanded by her parents. But it did not change anything. She ended up self-injuring, not considering herself punished enough.

Élianor reestablishes a form of spontaneous justice with her punishments. By injuring herself, she remedies the feeling of guilt and injustice that she experiences following her "mistakes." Here, the gesture takes precedence over the injury. In other words, it does not matter whether she cuts, burns, or hits herself, it is the wound itself that constitutes the punishment, not a symbolic or physical stake shaping the modalities of the wound as in the case of Marie or Cécilia. "Everything I could burn and put on my skin, I did," Élianor said. To my question about the places on the body she privileged, Élianor replied, "I didn't care, it was just whatever."

The evolution of Élianor's self-injury practice has been shaped by a concern for cleanliness. Unlike Marie, however, this is not about symbolic cleanliness, but about hygiene. Élianor fears infections: "Last year, when I think about it, I took anything, compasses, needles, and you can catch some bullshit like that. So, this year, I turned to razor blades and a lighter." Since the wound does not target any particular bodily sensation, but a sense of justice, the way of proceeding matters little: her only criteria is that she avoid infection, and that the degree of pain must precisely correspond to the perceived degree of transgression.

Purification Rituals

These four examples show the relationship between the stories of the self-injurers, the modalities of their practice, and the emotional system that makes sense of them.

Mary Douglas's classical definition of the notion of rite in relation to its efficacy reveals itself here to understand what is at stake. Douglas states that a rite not only exteriorizes the experience but also modifies this experience through the way in which it is expressed.[2] Indeed, orienting the practical modalities of self-injury allows Marie to restore a sense of symbolic cleanliness, Fanny to indulge and appease her anger, Cécilia to regain control over her body, and Élianor to satisfy a sense of justice. These young women perform emotional work[3] by searching for an injury method that would be adapted to their concerns. In other words, they modify their experience through the ways in which they express it.

More specifically, these rites restore some "emotional norm"[4] that has been, at least subjectively, transgressed. Marie feels dirty after an event related to rape; she then retrieves, partially, some symbolic cleanliness. Fanny feels anger in a context of widespread violence and an inability to communicate; she calms herself by the wounds. Cécilia, disturbed by her anxiety attacks, seeks to recover normal bodily sensations; the burns give her the impression that she lives in her body. For Élianor, her self-injury aims explicitly at punishing herself for mistakes and alleviating her sense of guilt. In each case, the participants' discourse relies on a normative system: cleanliness, civilized rules of communication, the supposedly normal way of feeling one's body, ordinary justice maintained by a good behavior. In fact, the emotions described reveal the internalization of (transgressed) social norms. Self-aggressive behaviors function as attempts to restore order.

Consequently, more than being rites in Douglas's sense, self-injuries look like what some ethnologists call "purification rites." The French anthropologist Denise Paulme defines this type of rite as the healing of evils ranging from the transgression of laws to diseases, by their symbolic projection onto an object or an animal. These rites are practiced "sometimes publicly, for the collective interest, sometimes (more frequently) in secret and for the purpose of private interest."[5] Manifold examples are reported by James Frazer in *The Golden Bough: A Study in Comparative Religion.* Frazer was one of the first to detail how rituals exist to project diseases or other evils on animals or objects in most cultures. The person who practices the ritual discharges her or his transgression by symbolically transferring the offense to an object or animal that becomes a scapegoat. Anthropologists have demonstrated that the forms of these rites, and the choice of what constitutes a scapegoat, are based on a symbolism stemming from the founding myths of the group.

Self-inflicted wounds are similar to purification rites in that they make it possible to switch from a state perceived as abnormal or deviant, to another state deemed normal. However, there are some important differences. First, the projection of evils is not directed toward an object or animal but toward the body of the affected individual. Secondly, the symbolism of the rite is not based directly on social rules stemming from founding myths but supposedly on individual spontaneity (unless we assume that neoliberal individualism is a founding myth, which is a possibility[6]). The participants indeed all related that they consider self-injury as an act committed by default, "for want of anything better."

The absence of external objects on which it would be possible to project one's evils calls into question the idea that young people who self-harm have psychological difficulties expressing their sufferings in ways other than self-injuring. This behavior can also be seen as a set of ritual innovations aimed at compensating for a shortage of "purification rites" in the social world.

I therefore put forward the hypothesis that people who do not have access to purification rites sufficiently meaningful to them turn instead toward their own bodies to rectify and amend perceived shortcomings or abnormalities. The corollary of this is that we must interrogate the way in which these rituals are made and unmade in our societies.

Part I Conclusion: Maintaining the Order

Injuring oneself to keep face. Hurting oneself rather than hurting others. Avoiding the display of embarrassment markers. Reporting conflicts on one's body so as not to disagree with surrounding people. Finding the best way to relieve oneself of an anxiety attack while remaining discreet. Anticipating the visibility of the scars so as not to disturb one's social relations. Discussing self-injury anonymously on the internet rather than risk being discredited. Expressing cleanliness, or justice. Experiencing normal sensations.

While self-injury is a socially stigmatized behavior, because it is a practice associated with mental disorders, it nevertheless allows a minority of people to preserve the fabric of interactions. It is a matter of power, in the sense used by anthropologist Georges Balandier: "Power serves a social structure that cannot be maintained by the sole effect of custom. The function of power is to defend society against its own weaknesses, we may say, to preserve it in order."[1]

In this sense, self-inflicted wounds are extremely developed power practices, facilitating the control of emotions that potentially threaten everyday life. As a result, they exempt practitioners from the control of these affects. When custom is no longer sufficient, these wounds lead to "defending society against its own weaknesses."

The daily practice of self-injury maintains a conservative routine.[2] Here, the order is not preserved by traditional bodies of social control (police, school, family, etc.) but internalized in the form of authentically lived emotions, which maintain the façade of order, and thereby discreetly realize the status quo.

Such an undertaking is not always successful, especially when people discover that one of their acquaintances self-injures or when a hospitalization occurs. In these situations, self-injurers react quickly, adjust their concealment strategies, and change the meaning given to their wounds. In all cases, they anticipate the possible reactions of the others, refining the sensations they seek, and envisioning substitution practices.

We thus realize that the concerned individuals are not totally acted on by their disorders, as if they were puppets subjected to their pathologies and to their youth as the depiction of self-injury as a syndrome suggests. Within their range of possibilities, they seek instead to adjust their actions to situations that they perceive as problematic. They prove to be "reasonable."[3] Although there are alternatives to hurting themselves, their use of self-injury nevertheless denotes a certain social discernment and exercise, and a certain practical sense in setting up their behavior.

Part II
A Social Positioning Practice

Introduction

How can we explain why some individuals, more than others, resort to self-injury rather than another practice? For some, self-injury has something more than other available behaviors. To use the language of economics, it has *comparative advantages* over other known practices that produce similar effects, though this does not imply that these advantages are the specific, conscious reasons underlying the decision to self-injure.

First, *potential discretion*. Self-injuries restore an ability to think and behave "normally," without the means of this normalization necessarily being visible. Admittedly, scars can be visible, but as we have seen, participants reported quite effective concealment strategies. And, compared to other equivalent practices, self-injury remains comparatively discreet.

Second, *the sensation of transgression*. Because self-injury is considered deviant—that is, considered as transgressing the norms of a social group, and thus socially stigmatized—it arouses a particular sensation of transgression. This sensation likely constitutes the "emotional shock" sought by participants, in a manner comparable to the thrill one feels when breaking even insignificant rules (e.g., taking the subway without a ticket).

Third, *deliberate self-aggression*. Of course, self-injury is characterized by its self-aggressive dimension. But, contrary to other behaviors involving the body (such as playing sports or eating), the direct attack on the body is the aim of the practice, which is not the case with other behaviors, including the most physically harmful. For example, in taking drugs, it seems that the attack on the body is a consequence, not that which is sought in the immediate future.

Wording the Evil

In the trajectory of those who self-injure, what gives meaning to this practice, which simultaneously is potentially discreet, provokes a sensation of transgression, and is deliberately self-aggressive?

Let us start with what the participants said. All but three refer to their family life as a decisive source of what I call their malaise: conflict with parents, violence, perceived communication difficulties, and so on. Whereas I previously used the expression "malaise" in its common understanding, I now refer to malaise *as a lasting emotional state that manifests itself, in the participant's accounts, by affects socially perceived as "negative" (sadness, anguish, despair, distress, etc.).* This state results in dissatisfaction with the ordinary experience and/or the social image of oneself. After family life, school life is the second-most reported source of malaise. Two notable discomforts arise from school life: stress related to success and a poor relationship with teachers or peers.

What can a sociologist draw from these claims? It would be reductive to confine oneself to only repeat these, accusing family and school of being responsible for the malaise. It would be equally reductive to only relativize these accusations, to minimize them as no more than the statements of teenagers and young people too lost and misguided to describe what happens to them. As for pretending to find a median point between these two positions, it would be unstable. It is untenable to disbelieve the participants too much and simultaneously believe them a little. This would establish a continuously faltering boundary between what would only be discourse and what would only be facts.

The anthropology of witchcraft can provide us with a way out of this impasse. Two of the foundational texts of the field, the investigations of Edward Evans-Pritchard among the Azande of Central Africa[1] and those of Jeanne Favret-Saada in Western France,[2] demonstrate that accusations of witchcraft give meaning to perceived injustices. These accusations make it possible to comprehend unfortunate events or misfortunes by imputing an origin to them. Evans-Pritchard offers the example of a man crushed by an elephant. We know that the elephant killed the man, but saying that the man was bewitched brings a further level of understanding, adding a *why* to the *how*. Sometimes, the origin remains inaccessible; this is the case for diseases affecting people or animals. Favret-Saada shows that the accusation of witchcraft is then a means of verbalizing injustice by referring it to a cause, a bewitchment or a curse.

Whether family and school life engender self-injury is not the question at issue here. We know that phrasing one's relation with certain persons (members of the family, peers, teachers) operates similarly to the accusation of witchcraft, in that it provides a possible way of articulating some issues and gives them a certain degree of coherency. What I mean is that this ongoing interplay between social situations and accusations has an effect that cannot be reduced to only the action of the accused persons. Rather, a whole configuration is at stake, one structured by what Hacking formulated in more recent terms as a "looping effect,"[3] making sense of the self-injury trajectory.

From this point, we can comprehend the social dynamics acting on the self-injury configurations and the accusations they are intertwined with, starting with an investigation into the historical context that conditions their possibility.

Historicizing Expectations

Why is self-injury given meaning through accusations against family and school life? Such an association stems from a specific sociohistorical context: in the nineteenth and twentieth centuries, family and school acquired new functions in Western societies.

First, family became the theater of emotional expectations.[4] Parents and children were no longer expected to only contribute to economic survival but were increasingly pressed to express feelings and care. According to some sociologists and historians, the contemporary family is also characterized by a quest for individualism: its members seek to realize themselves as individuals within its frame. The family is additionally regarded as responsible for providing an education ensuring social integration and well-being, which also emerged as a social norm in the second half of the twentieth century. This expectation especially affects mothers,[5] who are held responsible for the well-being of their children. Is it not a reflex, when a teenager feels troubled, to question what their parents have done wrong?

Regarding the education system, the emergence of mass unemployment in the 1970s in the West, and the general increase in the level of qualification necessary for employment have ignited tensions about what is expected from schooling. The schooling experience not only involves a relationship to knowledge requirements but also implies a set of judgments that foreshadow possible social futures, if only through the orientation of students within the educational possibilities. Regine Sirota noted in the 1980s that primary school pupils estimate their teachers' affection in relation to their own grades.[6] This suggests that the marks received, and all the other forms of assessment, have an impact on students at an emotional level.

It is therefore not surprising that at this historical moment when strong affective expectations about family and school arise, people may begin to express dissatisfaction with their experience in these two dominant institutions. Most participants consider that certain members of their families and aspects of their school life have failed to provide them with the means necessary to achieve minimal self-fulfillment. The expectations of self-fulfillment and its role in broader spheres of society cannot be understated.

Positioning Oneself

Our initial question becomes more elaborate. Which mechanisms make meaningful the adoption of a potentially discreet self-aggressive practice that provokes a sense of transgression in the practitioner and is enacted in response to dissatisfaction toward family and school?

Early in the initial interviews, most participants designated their family life as a direct cause of their malaise. I asked them to develop this point, inquiring into the "personality," occupation, and educational background of their parents and grandparents, as well as probing further into their relationships with their siblings and their family in general. Interview after interview, it became clear that issues of social positioning were central to the participants narratives. Noting the centrality of issues pertaining to social positioning, I hypothesized self-injury as a social positioning practice.

By "social position," I mean (in a broad sense) the way in which individuals position themselves within the society they live in. This concept has two dimensions: first, the "objective" position—the place objectively held by individuals in the social world (depending on their social class, gender, etc.). Second is the "subjective" position—the way individuals perceive their position in the social world.

By extension, the notion of social positioning denotes a dimension of activity whereby individuals negotiate their (objective or subjective) social position. This negotiation may involve adjusting to it or attempting to develop it, intentionally or not, purposely or not. This conceptualization of social positioning aims to provide a finer account of the relation between individuals and social stratification than the usual accounts of their position through quantifiable variables—such as level of education, economic capital, and so on—or discourse on subjective positioning—such as the expression used to qualify one's place in the social space.

Ultimately, if I have been led to conceive of self-injury as a practice of social positioning, it is because, during the interviews, most of the participants asserted a link between their self-harming behavior and their difficulty in managing the repercussions of their and their family members' social position on their lives. These repercussions were embodied in their everyday family and school lives.

In the second part of this book, I will show this connection in detail, following the three comparative advantages previously distinguished: the potential discretion (chapter 7), the sensation of transgression (chapters 8 and 9), and the deliberate self-aggression (chapters 10 and 11).

Notes for the English Edition

As most of participants of this research grew up and live in Francophone Europe, it is necessary to question whether some differences may exist regarding social positioning, especially when comparing France with the United States. Numerous studies have addressed social stratification and education in both countries. We know that Western countries are stratified, where stratification implies economic, cultural, and symbolic inequalities affecting the everyday lives of people. In both France and the United States, a beliefs regarding "class fluidity"—that there are no longer inequalities in opportunity—has developed. It is likely that this belief in equal opportunity is exaggerated in the American context; after all, it is the birthplace of the "American dream." But data consistently shows that while opportunities for mobility have generally increased throughout the twentieth century, there still exist strong social reproduction patterns in both countries. Moreover, it has been suggested that the impression of greater social fluidity mostly reflects the changing structure of work (the increase of skilled jobs in the work market), not the changing structure of opportunities.[7] Consequently, the tensions revolving around upward social mobility found in the narratives of the French interviewees are very likely to resonate with the experiences of everyday Americans.

Regarding the French and US tertiary education systems, we may assume some differences. The French system is centralized and cheap;

the cost for attending an undergraduate program is generally US$200 per year and US$270 for most postgraduate programs. In comparison, the US system is decentralized and very expensive. This suggests that despite similar patterns of inequalities, the modes of distinction operate differently. In particular, economic capital would relatively play a greater role in the educational opportunities of American youth.

In addition, those in France and the United States who have experienced some upward social mobility, have proffered different conceptions of this process. Jules Naudet's comparative study thus shows that mobile French people tend to underscore a feeling of isolation when discussing their trajectory, or at least a feeling of not belonging regarding both their original class and that to which they have ascended. In contrast, mobile Americans emphasize feelings of pride and recount little-to-no significant tension regarding their former or current classes.[8] There is an American cultural narrative valuing success, which is less prevalent in France. This difference may also be partly explained by a generational gap, stronger in France than in the United States. In the French context, statistically speaking, baby boomers have been widely privileged by the welfare system, while in the context of the United States, less inequalities exist in the generational distribution of wealth.[9] This explains, for example, a greater common understanding between different generations in the United States. More generally, however, the psychological costs associated with social mobility that Bendix and Lipset pointed out in the 1950s continue to be reported in current inquiries.[10]

Consequently, with a few possible variations, the social processes underlying the stories presented in the following are not particular to the French context. My "discovery" of the relation between social positioning issues and self-injury, and its originality to the current literature, likely stems from my training. I was trained and socialized in an intellectual milieu where few distinctions existed between sociology and anthropology.[11] This has enabled me to deploy insights from the anthropology of kinship, which traditionally proposes a more configurational approach composed of extensive kinship studies based on genealogies and multiple interviews. This differs from conventionally sociological studies of the family, often grounded in one-shot interviews regarding the meaning of the family in everyday life. Moreover, the influence of Pierre Bourdieu plays a significant role in the French academic environment. Bourdieu's influence has particularly sensitized French academics to social positioning issues beyond the usual quantitative variables generally employed to measure inequalities, allowing to approach social positions as flexible social features involving emotions, self-feeling, meanings, relations, and aspirations. In sum, the combination of this anthropological and Bourdieusian legacy with the Goffmanian perspective on the nature of the interaction order constitutes the theoretical and methodological ground of the analytical model that follows.

7 The Staging of Discretion

"Staging discretion." At first glance, the expression appears contradictory. To be discreet seems to suggest *not* staging oneself, to maintain a low profile. But, actually, to remain discreet is to stage the ordinary, to secure a "normal" appearance. A large proportion of participants self-injure to maintain this routine, as a backstage activity—or as Goffman would say, aiming to keep face in public, and particularly within the family.

Three eloquent cases, those of Louise, Clémence, and Elsa, enable us to understand the mechanisms by which these young women came to have, or want, to regulate their emotional state in a potentially discreet way. Their stories were chosen because they help us understand some striking features in the data collected. These include the similarity of issues, such as expectations of social mobility within families, and the different operations of such issues in different families. For instance, Louise and Clémence are expected to continue their families' upward social mobility initiated by their parents, while Elsa is expected to reproduce the ascension achieved two generations ago with the successful career of her grandmother.

In the second part of this chapter, discretion will be addressed regarding school life, in the case of "good pupils." Most participants experienced highly successful schooling. I will show how, in these cases, the issue of discretion emerging in family life prolongs itself in school life.

Louise: "Everyone Had a Place and I Had None"

I contacted Louise through a forum, and we did an interview by instant messaging, then another face to face. The young woman is also the author of an autobiographical book, which provides additional information about her personal history—which we will keep anonymous. The only daughter of two retired schoolteachers, she was twenty years old at the time of our first interview. She studies Modern Literature by correspondence while preparing, as an independent candidate (i.e., without any preparatory training, as students usually do), for the very selective competitions to enter one of the most elite university curriculums in France. As an excellent student—the top of her class—she explains to me that involvement in her schoolwork is a "means of escape."

Louise experienced an intensive period of self-injury from the age of twelve, when she began little by little, until she was nineteen. At nineteen she ceased self-injuring regularly, but has episodic relapses. According to her, her malaise largely results from the abuses inflicted by her maternal grandfather (now deceased) when she was a child. He raped and tortured her for several years in the family home where he also lived. She also notes that her parents turned a blind eye to these facts. Louise points out that it is unlikely that these acts (sexual abuses in her room, confinement in the cellar of the house, etc.) could have unfolded without them noticing. But the other sources of her malaise varied, which she recounts during the interviews: "I felt ill at ease, I was very shy, very alone, I did not reach out to the others, my mother regularly insulted me."

Very quickly, our discussion turns to the theme of family issues, most notably, that her relationship with her mother has always been characterized by conflict. According to Louise, her mother frequently belittles her. She describes her father as "a shadow, who shuts himself in his office at the slightest sign of conflict." The absence of support from her parents in a context of incest is the main cause of this family discord, which manifests itself daily by silence.

[Instant messaging]

INTERVIEWER: When you went to the hospital [after cuts requiring stitches] you left school alone?

LOUISE: When it went too far.... In general, sometimes I would tell my father, "I need to go to the hospital," too. He said, "You piss me off," but he took me there. There was a very heavy atmosphere in the car.

INTERVIEWER: Uh ... there I have trouble understanding. You were telling him why you wanted to go to the hospital?

LOUISE: He knew I cut myself when I was fifteen, so I didn't need to say why. My parents knew, but we did not talk about it. And they did not react except when I said, "I have to go to the hospital."

INTERVIEWER: Ah ... but you did not talk to your parents about what happened, even a bit later?

LOUISE: No, well, they always knew, but we never talked about it. We never spoke in my family, never. Especially not about sensitive topics. Everything was based on appearances, and my parents did not want to harm their image.

INTERVIEWER: Why are they so attached to their image?

LOUISE: Difficult to say ... at home, everything is based on good appearance ... I believe that for them, it's a way of denying or refusing their responsibilities and certain actions that have contributed to destroying me [allusion to the passivity of her parents when her grandfather abused her] ... and incidentally a way of making me look like the wicked one: "Look, what she says is false, we have a good image."

The silence around Louise's self-injury and the sexual abuse she suffered maintains the daily order of family life. Other reasons for this noncommunication appear quickly:

[Instant messaging]

LOUISE: I also know that I was always told at school / middle school / high school that I was brilliant, and that my mother could not tolerate the idea that I might be more than her (my father was following my mother all the time).

INTERVIEWER: Did your mother study too?

LOUISE: Yes, but she is a primary school teacher, and to her, it's hyperdemeaning work. And she has an inferiority complex because her brother graduated at Polytechnique [an elite engineering university in France], and earns more than her also, I think.

INTERVIEWER: Ah ... what would have she wanted to be, your mother?

LOUISE: I don't know.... Hold a higher status. Belong to "high society." Earning more money above all.

This excerpt of the interview suggests that in Louise's family, the attention paid to their image originates from her mother's feeling of inferiority; an assumption confirmed when Louise evokes her position (as she represents it to herself) in her extended family: "And I'm the youngest in my family. I have cousins on my mother's side [the sons of the polytechnician] who are ten years older than me. If you will, when I was born, it was made clear to me that everyone had one's place already, and that I had none. I was, quote, 'the pain in the neck,' and 'the dirty little bitch.' [instant messaging].

Louise and her parents suffer the backlash from the upward social mobility of the engineer uncle. Her mother refuses to accept a relative downgrade in her occupation compared to her brother's, and reacts by preserving a "good image," an appearance that would place her, in the eyes of the others and herself, at the same level as her brother. Louise's mother's attention to the defense of her image—a symbol of an expected social position—appears throughout the interview, especially so when Louise explains her mother's brutal decision to cut all contact with her husband's family. According to her, the social position of her paternal grandparents does not correspond with the expected image; they are "cow breeders from generation to generation."

Louise's denunciation of this situation refers to the place she holds in the extended family. Younger than her maternal cousins, born of a relatively less prestigious lineage, she feels that she has no place, that she is excluded for no reason. The sexual abuses and the self-injuries (the latter a result of the former in her parents' minds) arouse neither empathy nor understanding. For Louise's mother, admitting these problems amounts to losing face—something entirely unacceptable. Louise sees herself not excluded in the proper sense but as being subjected to self-presentation imperatives that amount to a form of symbolic exclusion. She is encouraged to suppress the memories of incest and incited to succeed socially. Tension between the parallel expectations to succeed and to not succeed is summarized by the attitude of her mother vis-à-vis her studies. During her high school years, Louise was regularly told that she would never earn her degree. At the same time her mother pushes her to follow the scientific path, which she considers more promising.

In view of her unfavorable family position, the feeling of extreme devaluation and loneliness reported by Louise makes sense. Self-injury is one of the ways for Louise to react by imposing a balance of power. If someone were to discover her scars, or know that she consulted a psychiatrist, or learn what her grandfather did, her parents' entire reputation would be affected. Louise thus finds—despite herself—a way of positioning herself and having a certain hold on these prestige relations, which overwhelm her.

Clémence: "You Don't Have the Right to Feel Bad"

As with Louise, I contacted Clémence via the internet and, a few weeks after our initial contact, conducted a face-to-face interview at her home. Clémence, twenty-four years old at the time, is studying sociology at the master's level.

She has been experiencing eating disorders since her teenage years and began to self-injure at the age of nineteen. Initially conceiving of this practice as a form of suicide training, she now associates it with other self-aggressive behaviors, such as excessive drinking and "destructive" sexual relations, that is, sexual relations with people with whom she does not really want to have sex—which gives her the impression of "treating myself like a whore."

She explains her malaise through the difficulty she encountered in maintaining social relations. This difficulty sometimes plunges her into a solitude that she traces back to childhood. Her parents would often come home late from work, and she found it difficult to build friendships at school. With the feeling of not having a place, of being—in a certain sense—surplus, both regarding certain social situations and in a broader, more existential perspective, Clémence struggled to find meaning in her existence. Later, she was the victim of a rape that deepened her malaise. As in our first interview, she relates the feeling of not having the right to suffer:

[Instant messaging]

INTERVIEWER: It is weird that nobody around you noticed anything, because you weren't well at all?

CLÉMENCE: But they worried probably because I dressed more and more black and Gothic. They probably noticed. But in any case, we do not talk about it. And, anyway, I don't really have the right to feel bad.

INTERVIEWER: You don't have the right? Why?

CLÉMENCE: I dunno. Sometimes, you know, with the exams and all that stuff [the rape]. I wasn't in shape. But my mother, on the phone, I told her I was tired or stressed. And she yells at me: "And me, I'm not stressed?" And everything and everything ...

INTERVIEWER: And your sister?

CLÉMENCE: She has a similar personality to my mother. So she asks the question, but you'd better not be feeling bad if you don't want her to shout.... Kind of, sometimes I just say "hello," because I feel a little lonely and depressed and I get yelled at. Because she works a lot, and she is tired and stressed. And it's my sister, it's not on her to support me, it's me. My father is a little flattened and absent. Well, not really here like a father. A kid. And my mother sometimes yells at him and makes crises. Like we are all assholes, and she gets away and she cries and everything.

The informal prohibition of showing signs of malaise was accentuated when her father was diagnosed with cancer. She was twenty-one then, and decided to give up her suicide project and to slow the rhythm of her self-injury: "It was not the moment." Being the eldest sibling and believing that she has more responsibility increases the pressure that she feels.

As in the case of Louise, Clémence finds herself under constant pressure to keep face. Since her father's illness, she practices self-injuring in close relationship with the expectation of maintaining appearances. Indeed, they are "often ... linked to an accumulation of problems, of worries, which together seem difficult to manage especially that [she] is fighting and trying [her] hardest to smile, to look in shape and everything." Everything happens as if there were a quota of possibly communicated suffering. Her father's cancer would give him more legitimate reasons to display a malaise than Clémence. Consequently, Clémence feels obliged to redouble her efforts to look well and be stable.

This pressure on her image is associated with a pressure on schooling. Her paternal grandparents, who took great care of her when she was a child, give it great emphasis: "When my grandmother came to pick us up at school, the first sentence was not even 'Hello,' but, 'how are your grades?'" From a working-class background and having a low level of education, her grandparents placed a lot of hope in the upward social mobility of Clémence's father, Michel. Michel became an executive in the public sector, after having been a technician. This hope was even more important since Clémence's paternal uncle, who "barely works," did not meet the same expectations.

According to his daughter, Michel works very hard; he is a perfectionist. He represents a "little marvel" for his parents. But Clémence is now expected to perpetuate these hopes of ascension. At this point in her trajectory, her schooling focuses the attention of the paternal family, who seem to wish, through the academic success of the young woman, to convert what the previous generations have acquired through on-the-job promotions into institutionalized cultural capital.

Clémence's parents reproduce this pressure by insisting their daughter follow an exemplary school path. Or rather, as she formulates it, "they do not incite, they do not even consider the possibility that you won't pursue long studies." This topic provoked numerous disputes between Clémence and her mother. "For her, I cannot not do a PhD. It is not even conceivable." Despite her intention to pursue her studies as a PhD student, Clémence persists in making her mother believe that she will not do it, as a sort of provocation, which, for Clémence, preserves an independence from the path that seems compulsory: "When I ask her why completing a PhD is so important, when a master's degree already represents a high level of qualification, she answers: 'Because it looks good, it's a good diploma'" The image of studies "in the family, it matters," she says, before adding: "That is to say ... on my mother's side, they are ... very Versailles" [aristocratic].

Indeed, according to Clémence, her mother—unlike her father— grew up in a very "mannered," very "aristocratic" family. Clémence says that she feels uncomfortable in this context, finding it difficult to behave with as much class as them. Thus, for Clémence's maternal grandparents, her mother's trajectory is perceived as a downgrade; originally a social worker, she has undergone continual training to become an executive and is now the director of a rehabilitation center. Clémence's parents also settled in Brittany, in Western France. Such geographical remoteness and isolation from the Paris region provokes some disparaging remarks from the maternal "Versailles" family: "To them, they are yokels."

Here we return to a previously identified mechanism, that is, the attempt to compensate for a relative social downgrading over the generations by appearance and the application of pressure to children regarding their studies. This mechanism allows us to shed some light on the feeling of dispossession expressed by Clémence when, for example, she is asked about the choice of her studies: "Sometimes I wonder if I chose or not.... I believe that I let myself be influenced by my mother." Hence these emotions, such as the "desire to fade away," the feeling of not having a place, of being inferior.

She nonetheless takes on these family issues. When she works, her feelings of stress and anxiety illustrate the importance of successfully completing her studies. They also appear to be the basis of some of her self-injuries:

> [Instant messaging]
>
> CLÉMENCE: But there, today I can't anymore, frankly I have to work, and for that I need my mind.
>
> INTERVIEWER: What can't you anymore?
>
> CLÉMENCE: I can't think because the idea of self-injuring completely invades my thoughts.... I can't really do anything anymore. And he, he [her boyfriend] won't be happy. But I have to work. I'm not working fast enough.
>
> INTERVIEWER: Does it [self-injury] help you work?
>
> CLÉMENCE: No, but once it's done I don't think of it anymore. So it releases my thoughts, that's all, so it makes me more available at work. Less distracted ... it takes less time to self-injure than to hold back. And now I don't have plenty of time.

In her discourse, and probably in her daily life, Clémence oscillates between distancing herself from and taking on the family expectations for success. She adjusts her self-injury to the "productivist" line of action impelled by her mother. She self-injures to be able to work, to materialize her anguish while remaining discreet and silent, which is to say, by preserving the image of a girl who feels good about herself.

Elsa: Self-Injury "In the Rules of Art"

For Elsa, the practice of self-injury corresponds to a form of enhancing cultural capital. Elsa was twenty-two years old when we conducted an interview. She was studying for a master's degree at a prestigious Parisian university, renowned for its selectivity.

Her first cut dates to a trip organized by her high school. As she explains, "Being in a group is quite heavy, the atmosphere, you have to look good, you have to look good, to smile." She says that at the time, she was tired because of a diet that she had started a few months before to slim down, and that had caused her to lose a lot of weight. Her narrative emphasizes the importance she attaches to behaving well and to "look[ing] good."

In her history, the pressure exerted to succeed at school and the emphasis placed on her appearance is constant. She describes her father in particular as, "too oppressive." From the moment she entered middle school, he showed strong expectations toward her schoolwork. "He made me recite my lessons until I knew them by heart." To make him react, when Elsa was fifteen she faked running away and committing suicide. She swallowed about fifteen prescription tablets, while ensuring that the effects were minimal. She then left the house, leaving a letter that she summarizes as follows: "Do not look for me, I've swallowed many pills." She slept at a girlfriend's place.

Elsa's father did not study. He joined the public railways company at the age of sixteen, gradually ascending the hierarchy until obtaining a top executive position. But he grew up in an intellectual milieu: his father was a journalist and photographer, his mother a doctor. Although the family discourse encouraged him to become a lawyer, he initially assumed a downgrade in terms of cultural and economic capital, and then "caught up" with on-the-job upward mobility within his company. Elsa's paternal grandparents also closely follow the studies of their granddaughter.

Elsa's maternal family is a textbook case of upward social mobility. Her mother began her career as a primary school teacher, gained her diploma to be a high school teacher, and then became a *professeur agrégé* in French literature—an appointment that requires passing the most prestigious and selective examination for the public education system and that provides lifelong privileged economic and symbolic status. Her maternal grandmother also had an impressive trajectory. Coming from a family of farmers, she ended up as a professor of philosophy after completing the most selective studies possible in France. She often shows her pride for her daughter and granddaughter: "When she introduces us to her friends, she says, 'This is my daughter, a *professeur agrégé* in literature, and my granddaughter studies at Sciences Po.'"

Multiple pressures thus act on the appearance and the social success of Elsa. In the trajectory of her parents, social mobility represents more than the expectation of some standard of living; it has a strong symbolic stake. After completing her high school diploma, Elsa enrolled in the first year of preparatory classes for top-level French universities, a very intensive training known to require twenty-four-hour involvement. But she gave up after two weeks. This interruption was dramatic for her father. Elsa was not happy either, both for academic reasons and in view of her father's disappointment. By enrolling in the preparatory class, Elsa says that she wanted to prove her abilities to him.

She explains that she felt, until recently, dispossessed of these scholarly orientations. She wonders which studies she really wants to pursue. She highlights that her desire for success refers to her desire to inspire her father's pride. "I have a huge Oedipus complex," she tells me, pointing out that she takes on what her father expects given his own trajectory. A set of circumstances—namely, the trajectories of her family members—ultimately lead Elsa to locate the origin of her malaise in her family's expectations.

She started self-injuring in high school. Her parents broke up when she was in ninth grade, and she went to live with her mother. Elsa's father never knew about her self-injury practice. Although her mother realized that she self-injured, they never talked about it. Or rather, a tacit agreement had been established. Elsa being monitored by a psychiatrist reassured her mother; it became "useless" to talk about it. This silence is not perceived negatively; unlike in the cases of Louise and Clémence, Elsa prefers to maintain her image of a "girl who feels good." The meaning that she attributes to her self-injury turns out to be quite different as well.

[Face to face]

ELSA: I mean, there was also an aesthetic side, a side that I found aesthetic.

INTERVIEWER: The sight of the blood?

ELSA: Yeah, I found it really beautiful ... yeah, when I cut myself I always put on music ... beautiful music ... and dance, I did it, and I watched myself in the mirror, and I enjoyed it. Yeah it was ... [*laughing, embarrassed*] quite special.... But otherwise, I tell you, it was always very ritualized, always with the same music ... ah.... Mariah Carey! [*Laughing*]

INTERVIEWER: Mariah Carey!

ELSA: Yeah, Mariah Carey, always the same song.... "Without You" [*laughs*].... Then after, in front of the mirror ...

INTERVIEWER: Why the mirror? Because if you do it on your wrist you can see it.

ELSA: No, it was seeing me ... seeing my blood, seeing me crying ... blood, tears ... I thought it was beautiful, I don't know why ... well ... I found it really, I thought there was an aesthetic side.

> I found it beautiful, the suffering ... I don't want to be gory but actually sometimes I spread the blood on my face ... and ... that's it. [*Laughing, embarrassed*]

This "aesthetic side" has two functions. First, it provides the possibility of presenting a deviant behavior in a seemingly legitimate way and minimizes the suspicion of madness. Elsa specifies this aesthetic aspect very early on, which functions as a reassuring rationalization. Second, it establishes a genuine discourse of distinction. Thus, Pierre Bourdieu describes the choice of tastes: "For there to be tastes, there must be classified goods, 'good' tastes or 'bad' tastes, 'distinguished' or 'vulgar,' classified and at the same time classifying, hierarchized and hierarchizing."[1] Elsa uses the same type of categorization to describe her self-injury. When I ask her if she ever happens to injure herself more impulsively, she answers, "Everything was always calculated.... This is something that I found ... almost, I found it vulgar, I found it vulgar, to do that anywhere, no matter how ... in a compulsive way ... for me, I know that it was always in a mood rather ... finally a little broader, I don't know how to explain" [face to face].

She differentiates a "vulgar" way of cutting and a "broader" one, which involves something other than the mere wound—a kind of reflection around this practice. Another of her remarks clearly recalls Bourdieu's analysis: the rarity of a taste is, according to him, a form of distinction. As in economics, what is rare is precious. While most participants feel reassured to know that others self-injure, Elsa insists that, on the contrary, her taste is for scarcity. "The fact of seeing plenty of reports about it, I think it's not ... I mean, it rather encouraged me to do it finally, I don't think it's ultra-positive, I find it's not good.... One could say 'it's cool, everybody does it,' but I found it not good, I mean it's not funny. I wanted to be the only one" [face to face].

Elsa embeds her self-injury in a mechanism of cultural distinction, and our interview allows her to put the distinctive aestheticization of her practice into words. This behavior reflects both her difficulty in meeting the expectations of her family and the absorption of these expectations. That is, for Elsa, self-injury allows her to remain discreet and distinctive.

Self-Injury and the Trajectories of Family Members

Louise is somehow expected to repair her maternal relatives' social downgrading while extending the paternal ascension with her own success; hence the law of silence surrounding her sexual abuses and self-injury. Clémence also struggles with very different social universes (working-class paternal grandparents and aristocratic maternal grandparents). Each member of the family projects their hopes on her, which forbids her from showing any weakness, especially when her father fell ill. Elsa experiences similar expectations weighing on her, even if this process occurs in a different context, given that she has evolved in a more uniform social environment than Clémence and Louise and has a model of success—the exceptional trajectory of her grandmother. For these three young women, the configurations of their families build up an explosive sociological cocktail.

As we have seen, self-injury partly relates to the representation that each self-injurer has of the place he or she holds or believes to hold in his or her family. This place is configured through the play of the social trajectories that occur around the self-injurer. Often, the trajectories of both parents and some grandparents structure the perception of family expectations. According to these expectations, self-injury acquires different meanings: for Louise, a denunciatory opposition; for Clémence, an ambivalent silence; and for Elsa, a distinctive aesthetic.

Living Through School

As the expectation to succeed is found in many participants' narratives, it is therefore necessary to turn to their school life to understand how self-injury works within this frame.

The commencement of self-injury sometimes coincides with certain stages of schooling. Let us take Téo's story. Téo was thirteen years old and in the eighth grade during our first interview in 2008 (we conducted another interview in 2009). He is the son of a salesman and a housewife who stopped her studies in literature when he was born. Having been advanced a grade and always achieving excellent grades earned him a reputation of being "bookish" among his peers. To him, this label—which he understands as a pejorative attribution in his schooling context—prevents him from establishing satisfactory relations with his classmates. Téo decided to pull back from his studies, intentionally underperforming and straining his relations with his teachers by behaving poorly. His goal? To integrate. Relations with his parents became tense after a school meeting where his bad grades were accompanied by poor assessments of his behavior. His mother, he says, refused to talk to him for two weeks, because she takes this change as a personal offense.

In the weeks that follow, another parent-teacher meeting made the situation deteriorate. Many long arguments broke out within the family. The evaluations of his teachers began to mirror his relationship with his parents. Two days after the meeting, Téo began to cut his wrists. He explains that this was the only way that he was able to endure the pressure and incoherence of the competing modes of valorization between his parents and his classmates—a double constraint from which he saw no way out.

Caroline's story shows that in this type of situation, psychiatric follow-up can lead to a reorientation of family expectations regarding schooling. In our first interview, as we approached the topic of potential causes of self-injury, Caroline described the parental project: "I had to be among the best ones at school, to be the perfect little girl who does not speak back." This nineteen-year-old psychology student is the daughter of a physiotherapist mother, and of a father who wanted to be a physiotherapist but who had failed in college, taking on various jobs out of spite. It is probably not a coincidence that he asked his daughter to go to university after high school. Caroline enrolled, but did not like it. Feeling a growing malaise that she expressed through self-injury led her to receive treatment from a psychiatrist. This psychiatric follow-up helped Caroline's parents accept the idea that the following year, she could study at a lower level (e.g., by undertaking simple vocational training).

In these situations, the teachers acquire a status of which they are not always aware and of which they do not fully appreciate the importance. Their judgments, which define the degree of success of their students, also influence their student's relationships with their families. And when teachers develop more informal relationships with students, as we will see, they sometimes intervene almost directly in the trajectory of self-injury.

Stéphanie, a twenty-year-old sociology student, is the daughter of a parcel agency manager and of a special educator working in a social facility for teenagers. According to her, the pressure exerted by her parents on her schooling was extreme: "I was afraid to say that I had fifteen [on a test worth a possible twenty marks]. . . . It was competition between moms. . . . Which child would have the best grade?" Without realizing it, she addresses the issue of her emotional state exclusively through her schooling. Feeling a deep malaise in the tenth grade, Stéphanie explains this situation by referring to the optional course that she followed for four hours a week, a course she did not enjoy. But her difficulties, she reiterates, did not come from her school life, since her academic results had always been very satisfactory.

Her self-injury has instigated some special ties with some of her university professors, especially with a geography teacher:

[Face to face]

She told me I could talk to her if there was something wrong.... She said she could help me, and I didn't want to talk to her.... And one day ... one day, she sent me an e-mail, and I started to tell her that it was not going well, but I gave her no details.... And she told me that if I did hurt myself, we could talk together blah, blah, blah.... I didn't tell her, but she knew.... So, here it is.... Then she tried to help me, they all try to help me ... I remember, I was hurting myself at home, and college was the only place where I could be quiet.... One day I met my geography teacher, and I understood that she wanted to let me down ... I felt it like that.... She said she was not a shrink and that she couldn't help me.... I was angry because I was attached to her.... So, it angered me well.... I went to the toilets. I hurt myself.

The hopes that some students place in their professors continue to surprise me. They reveal a faith in school, and the intense emotional expectations invested in this institution and its representatives. It is as if, in certain family circumstances, the school was the only place where one might seek the sort of counsel usually provided by a priest or a psychologist; the sort of counsel that provides a sense of meaning to existence, a form of recognition and familiarity. According to Louise, some professors represented the only way out in face of isolation and the silence of her family.

[Instant messaging]

Anyway, one day I was in his class, I was just out of the hospital on a Monday, after a suicide attempt, and I cracked. I went out of the class and I cried, half covered under the radiator. At the end of class, I was not able to move, I needed to talk, but I thought everyone would go straight [away]. This teacher was the first to offer me a hand, he sat next to me, asked me what was going on. I said "Nothing," he said, "You're not credible," and he said, "You know, there are things that even an adult can't keep for himself ... a teen even less," and he concluded in saying, "If you want to talk I'm here." At that time, I had never spoken of the incest. A week later I gave him a confetti-sized paper with "incest" written on it, and from there I learned to trust him. He supported me all through my high school period, and I still see him when I pass by.... And one day something tremendous happened. I was sitting on the floor in this teacher's room, and he told me to sit on a chair. At that moment I hated him, but after, I realized that, in doing this, he told me, "You have the right to exist."

But whatever an individual's expectations are, all school professionals (teachers, guards, counselors, principals, etc.) are trained to detect situations of failure and indiscipline. The personal investment and the disciplined behavior of most self-injuring students do not fall into these categories. There is a problem here in terms of prevention: as long as we try to identify teenagers who perform poorly and exhibit undisciplined behavior, many of those who self-harm (including anorexics) will be omitted. And even when some young people are spotted, misunderstandings remain.

Let us follow Maya. During her high school years, she experienced anorexia, depression, and very pronounced self-injury, which led her to be hospitalized twice. Routine psychiatric appointments commenced on her release. After being trained as an engineer, her father ran a small business. Her mother is an accountant, working occasionally in her father's business. Maya pays close attention to her schooling and school rules. As an illustration, she wished to read the transcript of our first interview in order to monitor the correctness of her language. During the interview, she recounts the circumstances in which her high school's teaching staff spotted her malaise. From the point of view of her teachers, Maya's behavior was deteriorating; she participated less and less in class, showing herself to be isolated and closed off:

[Face to face]

In fact [if she met the principal] it was because of a class council, where all the teachers were talking about me. And "Maya, my god Maya, what's going on?" And she [the high school principal] used to summon all the bad pupils to her office, to say "Yeah, you're a bad pupil, what are we going to do?" And so, it was pretty funny because she summoned me too, but not for my results, just for my behavior, so I was in her office. And so, she takes her statistics, with the average of the class, all that stuff, and says to me: "Maya, so there is a problem with you I think, in view of your results, so there is a concern.... We can see this a little in your results." So, she starts talking to me: "Is it a school problem? Do you have trouble listening in class? Having difficulty following the lessons?" And so she comes out with my average scores, well above the average, and so she doesn't understand anymore why I'm here! [*Laughs*]. And so after seeing my name, "Ah, Maya, ok, that's something else!" And so she begins to talk to me about my worries…. "What's going on in your life?" blah, blah, blah … she tries a little bit to act as a shrink, and then she talks a little about herself.

There is a discrepancy between Maya's situation and the principal's discourse on academic failure and discipline problems. The principal can only fall back on two postures: that of the shrink, or that of the improvised confidant. If the school professionals do not know what attitude to adopt, it is because they associate good results with a form of well-being. This concept is apparently shared by Maya's father:

[Face to face]

When you have good grades, you are told: "No, you have no problem." It is like my father, so when I had to be hospitalized, it was before my final year in high school, there was the whole question of, "you are going to fail your exams." And so my father told me that if I were hospitalized I would fail all my studies. And there was the trick: "Listen Maya, why do you want to go to the hospital, you're doing very well, look at your grades!" It was always that, and it was like, "but really, but why, I don't understand, look, you have good grades!" And my father said this very often.

We can see how some good students who self-injure do not garner the attention of school professionals, whose attention is monopolized by the topics of academic failure and disciplinary problems. There would be students who do well because they succeed or who succeed because they do well, and students experiencing difficulties because they suffer or who suffer because they experience difficulties. Such associations (well-being equaling good grades) tend to constitute a system taken for granted in school institutions, converting, for pupils, teachers, and parents, the results of school evaluations as a measure of an individual's well-being.

"Doing Well"

Let us go back to the initial question. How would potentially discreet, self-controlled behavior be advantageous? Most participants complained about the importance accorded by their families to appearances: how they dressed, their self-presentation, or, more generally, their reputation. Similarly, academic success is highlighted to produce the image of a positive and prosperous family. In addition, some good students who self-injure do not pique the attention of school professionals, whose attention is monopolized by the topics of academic failure and discipline problems.

According to what the participants narrated, this situation is directly linked to a social mobility project carried out by one of the parents, consisting both of an expectation to succeed through schooling and to show this success through appearance. In short, the visibility of the cultural capital to be acquired is as important as its content. To question this staging would be to risk undermining long-term family work, exposing it to the danger of collapsing altogether.

In this type of configuration, because the practice remains potentially discreet, self-injury enables prolonging the family staging while simultaneously threatening it, for it can be shown or said that the practice then acquires a potential denunciation and discredit value. Injuring oneself becomes appropriate or intelligible if we remember the cases of Clémence, Elsa, Louise, Téo, Caroline, Stéphanie, Maya, and all those who could not be cited here. Their narratives show that different family configurations can produce the same effect: faced with the expectations of succeeding, of doing well and/or of showing and presenting such success, self-injury—as a potentially discreet practice—can make sense. Indeed, in these situations, is it not a reasonable compromise, in the eyes of those who self-injure, to have the opportunity of expressing one's malaise without making it visible?

8 At the Origin of "Relational Problems"

W$_{HY}$ ENGAGE IN a socially stigmatized behavior, while other behaviors with similar effects are known and socially admitted?

One possibility may be that, due to the individual's socialization, deviant behavior may be privileged precisely because it is deviant. The notion of "surplus emotional response," which Scheff defines as the emotional (over)reaction of a community toward transgressions,[1] can usefully be applied in the case of self-injury, provided that the emotional (over)reaction is understood from the self-injurers' own perspective. For instance, what if their own response to their own deviant behavior would provide them with the necessary emotional intensity to self-control?

Would it thus be possible to speak of a *predisposition to deviance*, in the absence of any deviant group or incentive, to explain this inclination toward a solitary form of transgression? This expression is not to be understood as it is in criminological discourse, where predisposition implies determinants or risk factors. I will rather argue that some specific social configurations may produce, in some individuals, a predisposition to deviance, in the sense that these configurations drive these individuals to consider themselves through a natural attraction toward transgressions.

This idea has been suggested by the following observation: many participants describe themselves as persons who are more inclined than others to behave "differently," to associate with other "different" people, and therefore to find themselves more exposed to "different" types of behavior. More specifically, almost all the interviewees reported that they suffer from relational problems. Since childhood or adolescence, relationships with people seem complicated to them, to the point of creating further behavioral difficulties in everyday life. This provokes the impression of being "different" or "out of step."

Individually, these statements hold no particular interest. But their recurrence invites us to look into them more closely, especially since this issue plays a large part, according to the participants, in the malaise prefiguring self-injuries. What does this repeated evocation of relational problems mean? Is it a simple effect of introspection? Indeed, it is not difficult to detect, throughout one's own history, certain challenges arising from communication issues. Is it a self-justification discourse? It may be tempting to justify in this way the enunciation of a stigmatized practice, making self-injury less embarrassing during an interview with a sociologist.

Do relational problems relate to a particular type of social situation? Can we explore the social genesis of these problems? Can we explore a social predisposition to deviance, in the sense of a configuration generating a certain discourse that holds oneself as being naturally inclined to deviance? I will pursue this last hypothesis, relying on the reading of Camille's and Marjorie's trajectories, because these trajectories are strikingly inverse, and their comparison helps understanding processes (such as relative geographic isolation), which are at stake in many participants' cases.

Camille: "I've Always Been an Elitist Bitch"

Through an internet forum, I contact Camille, a twenty-three-year-old Swiss woman. We conducted an initial interview via instant messaging before meeting for two face-to-face interviews. The daughter of a chemist, and a pharmacist, she studied linguistics at the master's level.

According to her, her malaise began at age fourteen. An argument with a close friend bothered her so much that after this conflict, she "ate almost nothing, [she] didn't speak to anyone." At sixteen, she became friends with a classmate who was self-injuring. When Camille figured out that this behavior "did her good," she decided to try it too, and "it worked well." So she did it again. This intertwining of eating disorders with self-injury continued until the age of eighteen, and persists today, but only periodically.

Camille explains the emergence of her malaise: in part, by a difficulty integrating with others, which she had experienced for a while, especially at school. For Camille, her self-injury was the result of a general lack of communication, and her wounds a kind of alternative method of expression. The history of her relationships with her peers opens further avenues.

[Face to face]

CAMILLE: As a child, I was pretty lonely, it didn't particularly raise any problem for me ... I mean I never really looked for another person's company. So I didn't like the breaks [at school]. I was bored shitless, but otherwise I don't remember being particularly sad about it. I didn't particularly want to have friends. And yes, around a little bit later, toward.... Yes, at the beginning of adolescence in fact, probably around thirteen or fourteen, there I, I also became more aware of other people's opinions, people's eyes and all that. I wanted more to have friends, there I may have suffered more from having trouble in.... But, I am an elitist bitch, so it makes me think that twenty percent of people are really big jerks and it's pretty annoying when you try to make friends.

INTERVIEWER: Since adolescence?

CAMILLE: I think I've always been an elitist bitch.

Camille clearly claims her "elitism." She found her schoolmates "stupid, yes, totally stupid:" "We did not have the same concerns ... I thought their conversations were stupid, actually it's, well we [Camille's family] never had a TV, actually. So, it's true that when you're told about the most recent popular TV series, last night's episode summed up—already if the series is not formidably smart, "you have to see it"—and super not smart when it is summarized by ten-year-old kids! So, it's true I was a little ... "yes, they are stupid they can't stop talking about the TV!" [face to face].

Her relational problems apparently stem from a feeling of superiority, itself engendered by a certain education, of which the absence of television is only one example. Camille's family is distinct in the great demands of academic results, and more generally of culture. This expectation is evoked in our first interview, when I ask Camille to reflect on the causes of her malaise.

[Instant messaging]

INTERVIEWER: And your problems were not only related to your ex-best friend I guess?

CAMILLE: No, it was the trigger

But I was very shy

And I had a lot of pressure at home

My father holds a doctorate in chemistry, and my mother finished her
pharmacy exams with an average of 6 out of 6 so I was obliged to
be intelligent:)

... I was always a good student and I had an average of 5 out of 6.

And I was in a German class, so I was doing all my classes in German
with German-speaking people while my mother tongue is
French.

Me I found [the score] perfectly honorable

But it is true that in working, I would easily have reached a 5.5 and
my parents wanted me to work to reach the maximum of my
abilities.

We are now used to this type of discourse. Camille's parents want
her to study medicine, but the project fails, causing tensions: "Ah, my
parents decided that we were all [Camille and her siblings] going to study
medicine! Unfortunately for them, no one did! But there ... Finally, my
mother wanted to push us to do medicine, and both [parents] are scien-
tists, so they would at least have liked us to do a scientific thing. When
we ... Finally, I remember when I told them I wanted to study literature,
they shouted quite a lot" [face to face].

While these high parental ambitions likely explain Camille's academic stress, and perhaps even shed some light on some of the origins of
her injuries, they do not provide much insight into her relational problems and her feeling of being different. However, the way she presents
her family's place in their village is illuminating:

[Face to face]

CAMILLE: My best childhood memories are when my mother taught
me stuff. One of my best childhood memories: I was a little
child ... we'd been to Vallon, actually, in the Roman under-
grounds, doing visits with museum guides ... and it is really a
great memory. So they [her parents] have always tried to teach
us a lot of stuff, so it's true that then I was pretty much out
of step with the other kids who maybe did not have enough
curiosity.

INTERVIEWER: The school in which you were when you were a child,
was it rather working-class, rather bourgeois ...

CAMILLE: So actually, it is the village school. It's a farmer's village, probably my parents were the only two people to have attended university [among] the parents of all my classmates. Yes, I think they were the only ones with a university degree. We're not even talking about a PhD.... And they were unanimously hated because my mother sent the teachers' memos back to the teachers, corrected. So already, initially, there is a discrepancy because my parents are already quite peculiar.... It's true that I understand that the teachers, after the fifth memo they received in return with the mistakes highlighted in red, and comments in the margin.... It doesn't look good. At the same time, they could also have made memos without spelling mistakes, it would have sorted everyone out.

Two doctors in a farmer's village. The family's sense of belonging is therefore limited and, indeed, they actively contribute to this as Camille's parents keep correcting the local teachers' memos, marking their social superiority. This causes some isolation:

[Face to face]

INTERVIEWER: Your parents, in the village, so, they didn't have a lot of acquaintances?

CAMILLE: No, but my parents are pretty lonely too ... in fact they have few friends.

INTERVIEWER: They have no friends from their work?

CAMILLE: [They don't have many friends.] They regularly see the parents of one of my ex's whom I was with when I was fifteen, with whom, for some reason, they get on very well.

INTERVIEWER: Oh, ok, and these people have a university degree, for example?

CAMILLE: Yes, they are very intelligent people, frankly I like them very much, they are ... really ... people who did not graduate as such, but who are interested in a lot of things, quite cultivated.

INTERVIEWER: And so, your ex was almost in the same situation as you?

CAMILLE: In fact he, Romain, was not in the countryside, but yes, it's true that he was also quite intelligent, and he was very ambitious, much more than the others. He also put himself, in a certain way, above the others. Yeah, he really saw himself at the top of the world eventually, and he was right because he made the Academy, which is a super reputable school, and now he's the boss of a bank in Liechtenstein, with an annual salary of ... a lot! So, I mean ... yes, he did well also.

Some people, however, are exceptions to this isolation. They are not formerly educated at a tertiary level, but they are at least cultivated. They share the same conception of culture and the same ambitions of ascension, as the career of Romain suggests.

Marjorie: "The Class Weirdo"

Marjorie finds herself in a reverse configuration. She is thirty years old, lives in Switzerland where she works as a special educator, and is very involved in one of the studied forums. Having discussed feeling different in a previous interview, I ask her to revisit this theme:

[Face to face]

INTERVIEWER: The last time we spoke you told me that you started to scratch, to throw tantrums ... when you were a child.... I'd like us to come back to this, because you were also telling me that you felt different from the others.

MARJORIE: I was quite out of step with the others. Since I was a very little child in fact, I mean, already when I was very little I didn't know how it worked, relationships, and so on. When I went to school, I was a little bit like, "What are all these kids?" Since I had been surrounded by adults—because, well, I am an only daughter, in the surroundings of my parents—it's rather ... so I had been surrounded by adults, I was very at ease with them, that is to say I was looking for the company of the teacher, when the teacher left the room I blew a fuse ...

INTERVIEWER: What kind of school was that?

MARJORIE: Well, it was a school in a relatively small town where there is a relatively bourgeois majority, and I was not really in the relatively middle-class majority. My father was a carpenter by training, and janitor during the holidays at that time; my mother didn't work, so we weren't rolling in gold. It's true that it was also a discrepancy, it was that there were a lot of my classmates ... I mean, the first time I went to the sea, I was thirteen. And I felt like I had a life that wasn't at all the same to that of my classmates, who were always leaving for vacations. But for just about everything actually, I mean, there were not many things about my life that looked like that of my classmates, whatever it was ... my parents' standard of living, where a majority of parents had a lot of dough, could afford a lot of stuff, which was very far from my case ...

INTERVIEWER: Did you live in the more bourgeois neighborhood?

MARJORIE: We were not at the periphery, but, in fact, the thing is that there is the upper part of the town that is really bourgeois, with villas, and so on. The bottom part of the town is much more mixed. So you have some really bourgeois stuff, just like you have pretty simple stuff. And we were downtown; moreover, I lived— which didn't facilitate my social life—right next to the school in an old house that was there ... I mean an old, small building, with three apartments. Yeah, an old thing, not very beautiful.

INTERVIEWER: Did you just feel like that, or do you remember some remarks of your classmates?

MARJORIE: Well I have memories, I mean ... remarks precisely in relation to the teacher who asks: "What did you do during vacation?" Everyone saying, "So I went to Spain, I to Italy, I went here and there." Me, "Hey, well I went to my uncle's." And there you have people who are like, "You never go any farther? Ah, have you ever been to the sea?" At last it was more of a sort of astonishment, a little of pity, I felt it a little like pity. A little like ... "Oh yeah, but at your place it doesn't work like ours."

Marjorie is therefore the child of a rather working-class family in a rather bourgeois town. The feeling of difference that she expresses is accentuated by her parents' age:

[Face to face]

At the age and mentality of the parents, because my parents were quite old, old enough to be my grandparents. So at the level of the values and the education that my parents gave me it's different, it was really different than what my classmates lived: regarding freedom, I had much less.... Yes, the choice of threads: kind of, for my mother, it was normal that she bought my clothes. And according to her tastes ... but not mine! Actually, not mine, but I didn't care about it at the time because I had enough trouble ... because yes, when you are dressed in pink with Mickey at school, when everyone starts to care about one's style, you are quickly bloody marginalized. So since ... already that, the fact that even in primary school—so I was nine, ten years old—my mother picked me up at school while I lived nearby, I could have done it very well on my own. All that, stuff like that, that my classmates saw me and said to themselves: "she is an alien."

These two cumulative parameters (social milieu and age of parents) give her the impression of being an alien, which is reflected in the attitudes of her peers. This feeling of marginalization is echoed, as it was for Camille, in her acquaintances.

[Face to face]

INTERVIEWER: When you were in primary school were you really excluded or....

MARJORIE: I had weird buddies. Frankly, in primary school, I was pretty well excluded and when I was hanging out, like in the playground or something, it was kind of with the other excluded ones. So, with a girl who was in my class and who had a slight physical disability, with a girl who'd just landed in Switzerland and who didn't speak French. Always those who weren't integrated. But that, it hasn't really changed actually! [*laughs*] We keep habits! Except that now it's really a choice, while before it was more of an obligation!

Marjorie alludes to her current circle of friends, which includes Camille, and is essentially made up of members of forums devoted to self-injury. All the individuals in this circle probably experience similar discrepancy situations.

Let us turn to consider Marjorie's self-injury. At first, it was bites and scratches.

[Face to face]

INTERVIEWER: And so, in what situation did these scratches and bites occur?

MARJORIE: It was often when I argued with my mother. Well, with my mother we always had a pretty bad relationship.... Because ... I mean, when I was a very little child, I don't think so, but ... yes as soon as I started to go to school and everything, there I began to ask for more freedom than what she wanted to give me ... that I began to say ... What often happened is that I began to grumble in saying, "Wait, with the others [students] it happens like that, and not with us, I'd like to be able to live like the others." And for my mother it was my classmates who turned me against her, at last it became the big melodrama each time.

The age and social milieu discrepancy disturbs family life. It permeates the management of parental authority; over the years, Marjorie realizes that she could have more freedom if her parents were like the others. She likely imagined that she could also enjoy the benefits of a bourgeois education. Marjorie expresses the difficulty of being socialized in two worlds with contradictory values: "I have some folkloric memories of my parents at school parties with the parents of a friend who were architects. My parents were trying to chat with them and, well … the hyper-refined questions … my father was far from being stupid, but not someone very refined … and you see on the face … pity … disgust … I do not know what.… And then I felt my parents were very dumb" [face to face].

According to her, the early years of middle school coincides with an improvement of her social relations. "It improved, but I was still the weirdo of the class, and I was a little more integrated. There were a few classmates who helped me integrate. Well, who came a bit from the same background as me, anyway" [face to face].

Marjorie's father died when she was thirteen-and-a-half. She had bitter memories of the many family secrets that surfaced when he passed away, especially those concerning his health. She reacted with agitated behavior at school, which became a place to let off steam. Her mother seemed to shut herself off, not wanting to go out of her home anymore, and insisting on Marjorie's constant presence. Marjorie found herself in a similar position to Clémence, namely, one in which family life rendered impossible the showing of any signs of malaise. As her relationship with her mother deteriorated, the pressure on schooling was further accentuated and the issue of her image in the eyes of others became the object of her mother's attention. "She was afraid of what people thought of her through me," Marjorie said.

Marjorie's malaise became progressively embodied. She gained a lot of weight and began to have panic attacks, during which she experienced strange and unfamiliar bodily sensations. "[During these crises] I really feel as if I am cut off from the world, not feeling my body actually, having really odd sensations in my body, not the usual sensations. I can't describe it. It's really a feeling of floating, of being disconnected, of not really feeling my body …" [face to face].

Self-aggression became the only way to calm these crises. First, during her teenage years, it took the form of punching walls. The cuts came later, when she moved in with a roommate who self-injured in this way, which inspired Marjorie. She then started self-cutting regularly, a practice that she continues to this day, though less frequently.

Two Reflecting Situations

Camille and Marjorie both experience a situation of local exclusion. Camille comes from a family of doctors in a farmer's village. Marjorie comes from a working-class family in a bourgeois town. Camille, in a position of social superiority, affirms her isolation by attaching herself to the elitism of her parents. At the same time, she attempts to avoid the path laid for her, by refusing, for example, to study medicine. Marjorie, in a dominated position, is totally opposed to the lifestyle of her parents, who sometimes embarrassed her. Moreover, Marjorie cannot successfully integrate elsewhere. These local configurations make them feel fundamentally different from others, out of step with their peers.

These two participants somehow pay for the residential choices of their parents: their relational problems become intelligible through the prism of the social discrepancies that result from their parent's residential choices. Maintaining distance from their acquainted social world, Camille and Marjorie somehow constructed themselves as "cleft habitus."[2] But the split did not lead to a feeling of multiple belonging, as is usually the case in these situations. On the contrary, it led to the impression of disassociation from others, or at least of non-identification with them.

In these cases, such processes of embodied, subjective isolation (linked here to the place of residence) explain the construction of a social predisposition to deviance, similar to that of other participants. To conceive oneself, from an early age, as someone who is fundamentally atypical, makes it almost "naturally" possible to resort to behaviors that are atypical and produce a sensation of transgression.

9 The Existential Crisis

THE PREDISPOSITION TO deviance can also be drawn from a frequently cited feeling: not having a place in the world. When they talk about their malaise, the participants evoke a loss of reference points, a doubt regarding the meaning of their existence. Why live? What is my place in the world? Who am I really? The social experience ceases to be taken for granted. One could theorize the existential crisis as the unveiling and the fall of *illusio*, to use Pierre Bourdieu's word.[1] For Bourdieu, this refers to an organizing principle of action, the belief that the social game is worth being played and that the rules are evident; by extension, that oneself is "authentic" in following them.[2]

Unlike Camille and Marjorie, whose narratives are marked by a series of distinct stereotypes (intellectuals and farmers, proletarians and bourgeois, etc.), Vanessa does not provide similarly clear leads to identify the social dynamics of her malaise. Of my sample, Vanessa's case is the hardest to interpret within my analytical frame, which is why I consider it after having dovetailed Camille's and Marjorie's stories.

This difficulty is not due to a lack of reflection, or a paucity of words. Despite only conducting one face-to-face interview, Vanessa and I exchanged many emails, and she took full advantage of the written form to deepen certain points and bring up new topics of conversation. In addition, she sent me a text of about ten pages, which she had originally written without the intention of it being read, and which recounts this period of her life when she felt bad and began to self-injure. Confronting one of the most mysterious stories of this research will enable us to sketch further hypotheses regarding the social predisposition to deviance.

"I've Always Been Shy"

When I met her, Vanessa was twenty years old. She lived with her parents, both of whom are social workers, and her brother, who is two years younger than her and who is undertaking vocational training. Her father comes from a working-class background and taught in high school before becoming a social worker. Vanessa's mother is the daughter of a skilled factory worker and a seamstress. She describes her maternal grandparents as more cultivated than her paternal grandparents; their interest in culture is linked to the syndicalism of her grandfather, a fervent communist activist.[3] Vanessa's two parents are thus in a position of slight upward social mobility, in comparison to their own parents. This mobility is not linear for the father, who has undergone an intragenerational downgrading by ending his career in education; whereas it does appear linear for her mother, given that she was probably encouraged to study by the maternal grandfather. Her maternal grandfather also constitutes a potential "ally in ascension" for Vanessa.

The family lives in Brittany, in a "district of villas," inhabited mostly by the middle class, according to Vanessa. However, the term "villa" suggests that the district gathers people from the upper-middle class. Therefore, she finds herself in a situation of social subordination in relation to the socioeconomic composition of the neighborhood's residents, which weighs on the family management of the image.

[Mail]

I remember when we were little we had to go.... Every night during the month of December we had to go to some people's place for a drink or stuff like that and then once, my brother and I wanted to go there before our parents, because there were friends of ours in the house. And then we wanted to leave and my parents said, "no, no, you wait for us, we must arrive together because we must appear as a united family." So, well, we laughed a little bit because it was ... I mean it's not necessarily representative of what always happens!

This slight social discrepancy vis-à-vis the neighborhood is less structuring than it is, for example, for Camille and Marjorie. When Vanessa tells her story, she distinguishes her childhood and adolescence. Childhood is presented as a carefree period in the family, although she describes some pronounced shyness at school, which will later contribute to her adolescent malaise. Here is how her autobiographical text, entitled "Endless Story," begins:

As far back as I can remember, I have always been shy.
My first two years of school exposed me to others. I had a few friends with whom I played a lot, but some kids had fun bothering

me. I remember in particular two girls of my class, older than me, and a "big guy" from the classroom in front of mine, for whom it was not difficult to frighten me, a single "boo" was enough.

I was happy at home, but at school, I was not very sociable. Over the years, I had some real friends, not many, and quite a lot of time spent with the excluded group, or very superficial relationships with the others.

She places emphasis on her relational problems since childhood. Regarding what we have already discussed in other cases, there is nothing new here; Vanessa bluntly attributes this shyness to her education. According to her, the family atmosphere is characterized by the scarcity of conversations and the difficulty of exchanging ideas: "In the family, let's say ... we never had good communication, actually. I never say when things are not going well, for example." She presents these relational difficulties as a driving force for many of her worries, for example associating how she manages her affective relationships with her education.

[Mail]

During the interview you asked me what happened when I was arguing with my boyfriend. I do not know anymore what I answered, but in fact, we were not arguing. I did not say anything when something was wrong, I cried at night when he was sleeping, I often wanted to cut myself, but I did not want him to see it, so I held back. I did not want him to know that it was not right for me. And the few times I tried to tell him things, I felt I was not listened to. It is a lack of communication that comes from my family.

Vanessa does not explain this perceived lack of family communication. She talks about her parents' fear of "anything that is not slick," by which she means any relational encounter that is not smooth. Her parents, social workers, were terrorized (especially her mother) by the idea that their children would become like the people they supported. They therefore endeavored to ensure that Vanessa and her brother saved face and expressed themselves in a way that did not make them look like the social cases encountered in their professional life. It is very likely that the perceived lack of communication would come cumulatively from the moderate social mobility of parents (which is prolonged through the expectations toward their children), and the modalities of their work (they are regularly confronted with people in situations of great difficulty, an image, above all, of what not to be).

Becoming a Teenager

[Autobiographical text]

The summer when I was sixteen, childhood left me, little by little; I discovered the boredom of adolescence, much deeper than the boredom of my younger years. I realized that something was wrong in my life. I was trying to understand myself. I believe that these summer holidays were the longest of my life. I was looking for answers to my loneliness. I needed to communicate, I needed to be someone. Yet, I spent my evenings in my room, listening to the radio or music, writing, drawing, occupying my nights of insomnia, between depression and agitation.

This summer is a turning point for Vanessa. Her shyness and her communication difficulties provoke a sense of isolation, which she does not bear well. She would like to enjoy friendly relationships. The desire to leave grew stronger.

[Mail]

I always want to leave. I always feel that I do not really live my life, that it's just something "in waiting," "to pretend," but I don't know exactly in waiting for what.... I lived another life in my head, and I wanted it to become reality.

Often, I thought I would have preferred not having a family, no parents, no one attached to me. Because I had the impression of showing a false image of myself to everyone, an image that suited others, by fear of taking on what I wanted to do, who I wanted to be.

These lines express a form of disarray that we could find among many adolescents: the impression of not living one's life, of having to pretend, distancing oneself from the *illusio*, from the expectations that shape social life and give it meaning. This existential crisis seems to stick ever more in the mind of Vanessa.

She then experiments with some self-aggressive behaviors that offer a response to her confused questions by diverting her attention. On a day of boredom, she starts playing with needles, "like a game." The memory of two girls she knew, whose arms were injured, and a sudden attraction toward this behavior, as well as the opportunity to integrate into a forum, motivate her to continue. Being attracted by this forum—a very rarely encountered pattern of entry into the self-injury trajectory—favors a transition that usually occurs during adolescence. Namely, moving from family and school socialization to socialization within the peer group. And since self-injury refers to the imaginary of adolescent malaise, it offers the individual who practices it a social role other than the one offered by the traditional institutions of school and family. The posture of the suffering adolescent resorting to a deviant practice to express their malaise is probably more attractive than the one of the shy and lonely child.

The Runaway

On the internet, Vanessa meets some people with whom she gets on well, and ends up building some lasting friendships. At the same time, she self-injures daily, but daily life becomes problematic. Her malaise is compounded by a decline in academic performance and deteriorating relationships with teachers and other high school students. When schoolwork was due for submission and class presentations required, Vanessa was overwhelmed with stress. She describes her experience as unlivable.

An event then comes to mark her trajectory: she runs way. She performs her escape after long mental—and without much material—preparation. She recounts it at length in her autobiographical text.

> And the back-to-school season arrived, the last year before the high school diploma. I held up, my parents still did not see anything, and that suited me perfectly. My dream of another life was being built more and more in my head, until the idea of running away, the realization of which had been precipitated by some school events.
>
> It was also the time when I "met" Marc on the web. He was a boy from Toulouse, shy, sensitive, and a little weird. I felt we were alike. I told him about my idea of running away, and he also wanted to leave home. We made some plans, but none of them succeeded. I left alone.

Vanessa distinguishes between the world of adults, against which she remains silent and discreet, and a world in which individuals like Marc exist, providing common ground for mutual understanding. "Shy, sensitive, and a little weird": we have seen these adjectives in the narratives of Camille and Marjorie who, in their impressions of being different, similarly claimed to have sympathized only with people resembling them. As for Vanessa, the day of her runaway has come.

[Autobiographical text]

Eighteen years old and a few months, a Wednesday. It had been a long time since I wanted to leave. My bag was ready. Not heavy, not much. A few clothes, two books (*The Little Prince*, by St. Exupéry and *Fragile*, by P. and M. Delerm), my cell phone, my notebook, a few drawings and pens to continue them with, and a couple of things I have forgotten.

The causes of my running away have always been blurred for others; for me they were clear, there were two, closely related. The reality, school in particular, was unbearable for me and I had this imperative need to flee. On that day, I had to do an important piece of schoolwork—I had done nothing. On the other hand, I dreamed of another life, believing that I could get closer to it by moving away from my real life, the one that I did not like. This fleeing was only a stage, the culmination of a period of malaise, the beginning of another one, a crisis.

She leaves one morning and finds herself in front of the local train station. She does not know where to go. One of her friends, Paul, agrees to host her. She stays three days at his home and appreciates being able to openly talk to him about her malaise.

[Autobiographical text]

I did not know where to go and I was afraid. But I was not alone. He consoled me. For the first time in my life, a friend took me in his arms, took my hands, spoke to me with a soft and reassuring voice. For the first time I could cry without hiding. Speaking a little, and listening to him.

The running away is simultaneously presented as the fulfillment of her malaise and as an act of liberation, the possibility of finally approaching other horizons. Yet Vanessa did not desire any particular horizon. The end of this adventure inaugurates the beginning of a time of trouble.

[Autobiographical text]

His mother came in. She told that me she could not be an accomplice to my running away. That she had called my parents. Paul did not know. She said that they were here....

The world collapsed. I put my head on my knees. My arms over. I dropped my pen. I trembled, I cried.

They came in, with my aunt. My brother was also there, but elsewhere in the house. I did not move. I do not remember everything very well. They spoke to me a little. My father wanted to hold me in his arms. But I could not be touched. My aunt was very close to me. She talked to me. I managed to whisper, very gently, the name of Paul. She told him, he approached, and I asked that it only be the two of us. He asked the others to leave, they left. I could lift my head.

Later, an on-duty psychiatrist came. She asked me questions; I always had my head hidden.... She asked me if I wanted to go to the hospital. I said yes. Because I couldn't do anything else. I could not go home. She left.... We got out of the cars. My hood hid my face. I had no visual or auditory contact with anyone. But Paul was giving me his hand, and that reassured me a lot. I squeezed it, not too strongly, I hope, when we arrived.

This is how Vanessa ends up hospitalized in a psychiatric ward. Returning to ordinary life would take some time. She first goes out after a few weeks. An authorized weekend leave allows her to go to a friend's birthday party. At this party, she only meets people with a connection to the psychiatric world or to self-injury. Once all the partygoers leave, she refuses to sleep at her parents' place, wanders the streets, and waits for a shop to open to buy razor blades before going back to the hospital.

A few weeks later, her psychiatrists announce that her hospitalization is over. Again refusing to resettle in the family home, Vanessa stays with friends. When the summer arrives, and her friends go on vacation, she sleeps on the terrace of the family house. She waits until her parents go to sleep, so as not to give away her presence. It would take another two months before Vanessa relocated back to the family home.

"A Revolutionary with Nothing to Revolutionize"

By wondering about the dream of another life, about the opportunities and aspirations that Vanessa imagines for her future, we discover a void. Undecided, she chases after an ideal without an ideal in mind. She wants to leave but does not know for where. She wants to do something else but does not know what. She wants to realize her dreams but does not know which dreams are hers to realize.

We may approach this issue from another perspective: what models and ideals does the young woman have to guide her trajectory?

[Mail]

There is something I didn't talk about in my "autobiographical" text nor during the interview. I rarely think of it, it is a little hidden from my memory, besides I do not remember the details. Before going really bad, I think I was fifteen, I searched one day in my mother's office, when I was alone in the house. I found diaries, and I read, I think I needed to know what she had lived when she was younger, at an age closer to mine. I also found letters between my mother and my father when he was in prison (for conscientious objection to military service). In the early 1990s my mother had an affair, I do not know if my father knew it, but apparently there was some "libertarian" agreement between them at that time (I think this is not the case anymore since they got married in 1996). At that time, it shocked me a lot to learn that; I think I hated my mother. I thought that maybe my father was not mine. I remember especially a sentence that said that I was "the fruit of her inability to lose" my father, since she was in a relationship with him, but preferred her other lover. I cried a lot for that. I did not tell anyone, but I wrote it, and when I was at the psychiatric hospital in 2005, my mother insisted on talking with me over the phone, to tell me that my father was my father. She wanted to tell me about it, but I did not want to hear it. I believe that this discovery was one of the triggers of my malaise. Even today, I never talk about it, I rarely think of it, just writing it makes me feel a little bad....

What is a life ideal if not the transposition in a probable future of somewhat reworked earlier models? These earlier models, especially at the primary socialization stage, largely come from the parental lifestyle. Vanessa's discovery of her mother's affair shocks her, even though she is assured of her father's biological fatherhood, because it is precisely this element that reinforces the collapse of models (here conjugality) and her desire to run away. I then question her about what embodies her ideal:

[Mail]

I think that my father was a model, but not really my real father, my idealized father, the one of whom I read in the letters (he had written in prison), the one I saw in photos found in old carton boxes, young with long hair, traveling across Yugoslavia on motorcycle, or in South America. I was proud that he went to jail, he was a bit of a hero, because he had suffered from remaining faithful to his nonviolent ideas, by refusing the army (even if everybody did this at that time). I dreamed of the liberty of travel.

Traveling and defending nonviolent ideas. Nothing very original: who has not dreamt, at one point or another, of a more bohemian-like life? Nothing impossible either: why does Vanessa not commit herself to causes that have a meaning for her? Why does she not travel? This latter question is the most important one. Her daily life does not suit her aspirations. She wants to leave, to feel free. Usually, to fulfill this kind of aspiration, one resorts to travel, at least in the short term; or else, in the longer term, settles in another country. But for Vanessa, it had to be a running away, that is, an escape without warning, but also without anywhere to go except the apartment of her friend, at most, sixty miles from home, and always in Brittany. We are far from the South American and Yugoslavian paths that she fantasizes about in looking at her father's photographs. By her very indecision, her absence of ideal, the young woman upholds a "metaphysical revolt," as Albert Camus would say. Vanessa is aware of this. Hence, she qualifies herself, by analogy to a friend, as "a sort of revolutionary without anything to revolutionize."

Hypothesis One: An Indiscernible Social Mobility

According to Pierre Bourdieu, the degree to which an individual believes in the rules of the game that structure social life—the *illusio*—depends on the adjustment between their habitus and the environment in which they live.[4] Socialization makes it possible to embody some behavioral rules and representations as taken for granted. With existential crises, which Vanessa's story illustrates, there is apparently a tension in this schema.

To use Robert Merton's classical vocabulary of social mobility, one can distinguish the "group of belonging" from the "reference group."[5] Such a distinction enables greater understanding than the general and over-coherent notion of identity. The "group of belonging" refers to the milieu of origin. The "reference group" represents what the individual aspires to, the world toward which they direct themselves. Schematically, social mobility happens when these groups are different. It seems to me that the fall of the *illusio* may relate to some interference in the trajectory of an individual, at least subjectively, both regarding their group of belonging and reference group.

The feeling of not having a group of belonging is evident in Marjorie's case. She is sometimes ashamed of her parents, and feels out of step with the well-to-do children of her school. All this provides her with the feeling of an atypical social origin. As for Camille, she is very clearly on the side of the intellectual elite but her residential situation prevents her from fully living this position. Vanessa gives less information in this regard: she only reports being dissatisfied with her original lifestyle. One can assume that this may be linked to the status of her parents. Some research[6] suggests that this generation of social workers (trained in the 1970s) characterized itself by a strong "critical distance" vis-à-vis their social origins, whatever these origins are.

Moreover, the impossibility of picturing a reference group is embodied through difficulties in finding a goal, in obtaining a set of values, and in developing an imaginary toward which individuals can project themselves. There are two attitudes. First, Camille and Marjorie develop a critical perspective on most of the social environments they inhabit. As a result, they associate themselves with neither their group of belonging nor any possible reference group. Second, Vanessa fantasizes about an idealized life that she does not know how to define: she has no idea what her reference group might be; thus, contrary to Camille and Marjorie, she cannot criticize any specific group.

It remains to be understood under what conditions certain individuals struggle to represent their place and movements in the social space. This is a question that goes beyond the scope of this book. It should be noted, though, that the identification of a reference group constitutes an interesting avenue when one considers the means of quitting a self-injury trajectory.

Hypothesis Two: The Noncollective Framing of Malaise

Another common denominator in Camille's, Marjorie's, and Vanessa's stories—and reported in almost all the participants' stories—is loneliness and isolation, especially when entering adolescence.[7] Feeling out of phase with others, at school, in the family, and on an urban scale, seems all the more painfully experienced as there are no groups (neighbors, people in the district, etc.), or collectives (the extended family, for example) to make sense of this discrepancy. Where there could be "us" and "them," there is only "me" and "them." A persistent sense of abnormality emerges.

A quick comparison with the studied example of young people from poor backgrounds living in working-class districts is enlightening.[8] These young people are much more easily "localizable" socially: they stand at the bottom of the hierarchy of economic and cultural resources. Such a situation causes a malaise,[9] due to a foreclosed professional future and a daily life jeopardized by economic ups and downs.

Those who, despite such difficulties, succeed in going to university, still encounter significant disturbances in their relations with the different environments in which they find themselves.[10] The narrative of Younes Amrani,[11] a young man who grew up in a housing project in France, evinces the confusing conditions in which he finds himself when he is in his home district, but also when he tries to study and find a job. For our purposes, the significance of Younes' narrative lies in his description of the constant temptation he faces to engage in certain activities widespread in his neighborhood: smoking weed, practicing religion, hanging out down at the buildings, or committing delinquent acts. The young man perceives these temptations as obstacles to his will to succeed socially, but these also play as compensations for the socioeconomic difficulties people living in such circumstances regularly face.

Individuals in lower socioeconomic communities have at their disposal a large amount of illegal, deviant, or even socially accepted behavior that can frame the malaise generated by their social situation. While there are no longer strong common ideals or collective movements structuring life in the working-class districts (such as factory workers' sociability before deindustrialization), there remains a collective way of staging despair and adopting alternative scales of value, whether religious, delinquent, or otherwise.

What outlets exist for those young people who do not experience sociability in a sufficiently integrated group? What about those who do not know which milieu to connect with? They have no way of seeing their malaise framed and given sense by a socially homogeneous group. Vanessa is a perfect example: she is not attracted by a specific deviant behavior. On the contrary, she suffers from her loneliness, and seeks what to do by default.

This offers a lead regarding the gendered distribution of self-injury. Some studies in the sociology of education show that the sanctions punishing deviant behaviors in secondary school settings do not have the same effects for girls—who feel ashamed when punished—than they do for boys—who can valorize the punishment within masculine sociability.[12] Consequently, women—and young women in particular—are less likely to find themselves in situations whereby they can convert a predisposition to deviance into a form of gendered sociability.

From this perspective, self-injury expresses an individualization of the experience of malaise, which in certain circumstances, could be associated with an absence of deviant groups that offer alternative values and practices. Here we can draw an interesting parallel with the consumption of alcohol in the working conditions of the factory, as studied by the sociologist Michel Pialoux. Pialoux shows that alcohol is part of a collective sociability for the workers, while the foremen, who also drink, do it in secret.[13] In their hierarchical isolation, no collective can give meaning to their consumption. Similarly, no collective could give meaning to the malaise experienced by the participants of this book. In a certain sense, this situation makes it reasonable to resort to a deviant, individual, and solitary practice, such as self-injury.

10   What Gender Represents

Ana, a patient of the day hospital where I did part of my fieldwork, self-injured "only" twice. Still, I asked her to tell me about it. The teenager appeared skeptical; it seems that she agreed to take part in an interview with me just because she was bored at the hospital, or perhaps to show the staff members that she was taking part in institutional life. Our conversation was rather short. She told me that she inflicted two wounds, a couple of years earlier, with the intention of blackmailing her parents. She wanted them to let her go to Spain, and they disagreed. She wanted to highlight her point by showing them that she would feel bad if she stayed in France for the holidays.

As these first injuries did not make her feel anything in particular, she did not bother trying again. During our interview, she even insists that for her, hurting oneself is an unnatural behavior. Ana, who takes pride in her self-presentation and displays a very neat appearance, also asserts that she attaches too much importance to the maintenance of her body to enjoy this kind of practice. Ana reminds us that for most people, the mere idea of cutting or burning oneself is unthinkable, that self-injury cannot provoke in everyone an accessible relief.

Through what mechanisms do some people come to "appreciate" the effects of a deliberately self-aggressive behavior? I will answer this question simply: in order that someone *may* hurt himself or herself, they must first have defined their body as the place of their malaise— the embodiment of malaise.[1] In such a situation, the deliberate attack of the body may represent a solution, a way of providing relief to oneself.

The argument advanced in this chapter may be summarized as follows. In certain situations, certain social issues (subjective place in the family, expectations of academic and social success, residential configuration, etc.) particularly reverberate on the bodies of certain individuals. This occurs in such a way that these individuals may then associate their malaise with their body and turn to hurting their body to relieve themselves of this malaise.

The following examples show how such a process can take place through gender-related issues. The case of Élodie represents the situation among most of the participants. She describes her distancing from the traditional traits attributed to femininity and the associated gender roles. Furthermore (and this is why her story has been selected), she experienced variations in this distance, depending on family, school, and professional contexts. I chose to present the second case for the same reason as Vanessa's story, discussed in the previous chapter. It is one of the hardest cases to interpret, since Antoine develops an unusual discourse on masculinity. The third, and last, case is, somehow, the most radical example of gender distancing, since Tiffany, born and raised as a man, wants to become a woman. Developing these three cases will permit us to understand how the subjectively challenging embodiment of gender may be related to the practice self-injury.

Élodie: Having to Be a Woman

The story of Élodie—to whom we owe the concept of "postcoital downer"—illustrates well the possible transposition of social stakes toward bodily stakes.

At the time of our third interview, Élodie is twenty-two years old, and looking for a job after finishing a technical degree in commerce. Her professional orientation is not self-evident. Her family exerts intense pressure on her and her brothers' futures. Her mother, a special educator from a modest background, is especially invested in this project of upward social mobility. This is unlike her father, who is already endowed with greater social standing, having come from a very wealthy family and holding a master's degree in management. He is the former director of a medical-social institution and now a director of his own computer company.

Élodie describes her family as being uncommunicative with each other, the accompanying ambiguities of which likely result from a profound disparity in their conception of the future. Such disparity can be elucidated as follows: Élodie's mother, sensitive to all that affects social status and the family image, is distinct in her concerns from Élodie's father, who is more distant on this matter. The three children derogate these ambitions. Indeed, the oldest child, at twenty-eight years old, works as a plumbing-and-heating electrician, while the youngest sibling of twenty-four skips from discipline to discipline at university, studying in areas like philosophy that are allegedly not profitable.

Élodie paints a contrasting picture of her relationship with her father and mother. Speaking of her mother, she notes that they "cordially ignore each other." Their many disagreements stem from a divergence of their "vision[s] of things." Élodie summed it up as such: "Her, duty; me, pleasure." She describes the difference between her mother and her father as "day and night." "He respects us as we are, without wanting to control and modify everything," Élodie explains. We find here the same type of situation previously encountered: a family tension partly related to a difference in the social origins of the parents, which resonates on the expected trajectories of all the family members.

Élodie presents self-injury as her "mode of expression" since childhood. As a child, biting herself, or putting her hand under hot water usually helped her to calm down. This practice became routine from the age of thirteen. At this point, the young woman started hurting herself more "effectively" (her word). Élodie developed the habit of burning herself with a utility knife heated by the flame of a lighter. When asked about what happened the year of her thirteenth birthday, and what might explain the escalation in self-aggression, Élodie answers on instant messaging: "Adolescence. I am quite emotional, and I have trouble managing my femininity." How to interpret this remark?

Élodie asserts that she—once again—experiences relational problems. She feels uneasy in conversations with many people, while feeling fewer difficulties in one-on-one interactions. Furthermore, other relational events, such as frequent arguments with her best friend, prompted her self-injury to evolve at the age of thirteen. But these arguments underlie deeper issues. The best friend in question, very sociable and "cute," reflects the source of Élodie's anxiety. In contrast to her friend, Élodie does not present as the nice, cute, little girl her family wants. She sees her best friend as the stereotype of what her mother hopes her to be. The feeling of not integrating into this parental model gives rise to an ambivalent reaction: Élodie refuses to follow this model of the nice, cute girl, while reproaching herself for not wanting to incarnate it.

[Instant messaging]

INTERVIEWER: What do you talk about when you're with her [your mother]?

ÉLODIE: Uh ... "Ah, have you seen that I bought myself a new sweater?!"
An exchange that is all the more painful as we absolutely have not
the same tastes. We do not really talk to each other.

INTERVIEWER: You mean, about your clothes?

ÉLODIE: Actually ... she wanted to have a model girl, when I was little,
I had pretty skirts, nice nail polish.... And then, at six years old, I
said, "Stop, no, I don't like your clothes; no!" I nicked the threads
of my "bro" and that's it. From then, she had to do otherwise. I
wore the threads of my "bros." My brother, who is two years older,
we always had about the same size, even when we were very young,
his pants were too wide, but I put on a belt and there you go.

Throughout her adolescence, Élodie developed more and more frequent forms of bodily attacks. When she entered boarding school in the
ninth grade, she began depriving herself of food, not to lose weight, but
out of disgust with food. Her self-injury and eating disorders continued right up to the eleventh grade. That year, she says, her self-injury
practices diminished. This coincided with a change: Élodie moved to a
vocational school.

[Instant messaging]

INTERVIEWER: Why [did you feel better]?

ÉLODIE: My friends took me in hand. It was a high school of a
thousand pupils with barely forty girls. I felt more where I
belong; I completed a technical diploma in electronics, probably
my best years.

During her graduate studies, she again felt a profound malaise. She
writes during our instant messaging interview with a succession of abbre-
viations: "depression SI SA PH" [depression, self-injury, suicide attempt,
psychiatric hospitalization]. Élodie made a first suicide attempt during
her second year of vocational training (which she will repeat) by taking
a massive amount of medication. The reasons for this act are mysterious:
she affirms that she had no reason to want to die. The sexual abuse she
suffered, which she declined to discuss in any further detail, might have
occurred at that time. Her attempted suicide resulted in a two-week hospitalization in a psychiatric institution. Another preventive hospitalization followed a few months later. Currently, the young woman self-injures
periodically and irregularly, mostly during moments of tension.

The Staging of Femininity

To better understand the advent and evolution of Élodie's malaise during her adolescence, we must come back to the social dynamics of her conflicts with her mother. Élodie's mother wanted Élodie and her brothers "to be perfect, engineers, doctors, or lawyers, married at twenty-five, living in suburbs with children and a dog, a chic suburb, with a house and garden." She is eager to display a "good image of her family, her own success," which grounds her pressures on the schooling of her children: physical punishments (slaps and whacks) and an intense demand for very high grades. Paradoxically, by imposing these ambitions, the mother places herself on the sidelines. Her own comparatively low educational level is perceived to conflict with her insistence on academic excellence. Élodie uses violent words to describe and express this relegation.

[Face to face]

INTERVIEWER: What do you talk about with your parents?

ÉLODIE: Mathematics, computers, electronics, physics, chemistry.... My father is a scientist at heart, so he changed jobs ... opened a business in computing, and that's it. With my brothers, it's really around those kinds of topics. But if we start talking politically, or socially, or anything, we don't have the same opinions. And with my mother, usually she sulks because she understands nothing, feels excluded, doesn't understand, and then when we try to start a conversation with her it's ... Well I'm still the youngest, I'm twenty-two, I have a brother who is twenty-four, and the other twenty-eight, and she still takes us for children, so when she's still trying to impose her ideas, her way of looking at things ... it doesn't work. And even when we were younger it never really worked. In the family, so to speak, we are far from being dumb, we've always thought for ourselves....

INTERVIEWER: Is your relationship with your brothers better than with your parents?

ÉLODIE: Well, it depends. We have big clashes sometimes, but on the whole we stand up to them; actually on the whole we support my father and my brother against my mother actually. It's sad to say.

INTERVIEWER: Oh yes, your mother is a little ...

ÉLODIE: Dumb. It's unanimous.

Élodie's mother nevertheless holds a dominant, structuring position in the family. While her desire to ascend socially elicits rancor, it still constrains the young woman who defines herself, finally, in relation to this will.

The obligation to succeed shows itself through the body. The punishments that Élodie received during her childhood primarily gave a material—physical—consistency to this expectation. Also, that her mother wants to stage success permeates how the family members perceive their bodies. In addition to the model of the nice, cute, little girl, expectations to behave properly are many. The lifestyle to which the mother aspires for her children, which could be called traditional, requires a joint control of physical appearance and dress, conduct, sexuality, hygiene, and so forth. Élodie openly rejects some of these rules, contrasting, for example, the traditional image of marriage with a freer view of affective relationships and the rejection of sexual exclusivity.

But the most relevant prism remains that of gender. Élodie is said to be a "tomboy" since childhood, even if she resolved, from the age of eighteen, to "dress like a girl." Furthermore, she claims to have "trouble with girls on a regular basis, in general." Her experience of femininity, which she feels is problematic, sheds light on the links between her malaise and her relationship to her body, especially during middle school.

[Face to face]

INTERVIEWER: You told me that you had difficulties assuming your femininity for a while … did you also have this problem … in middle school, for example?

ÉLODIE: There, that's worse! In middle school, girls are like, "Ah, boys, they are so handsome!" "Have you seen how he is dressed, ah …," "I've been going out with Whatshisname since Wednesday!" [*Firmly*]. No.

INTERVIEWER: But for you, boys … I don't know, uh … they scared you at that time?

ÉLODIE: No, boys no … it was the boys who were afraid of me at that time! [*Laughs*] I have to say that when I started sixth grade, our English teacher chose where we sat in class, usually she put a girl and a boy side by side, and there I came across a guy who had fun putting his hand on my thigh … I told him once to stop, he continued ... twice, he continued ... third time, I took my compass and I stuck it into his hand. Obviously, it also circulated a little bit around the school so ... it didn't help my integration much.

Élodie illustrates feeling "off" around her peers, a very widespread motif in the narratives of the participants. She associates certain stereotypes of femininity with a level of cultural degradation. "I loved to read ... yes, and then people in general did not really interest me. I watched the others, but I didn't understand them too much, I never understood that fad where the girls had to look at all the boys and kiss them behind the hedges, I never understood" [face to face].

The message is clear. However, Élodie's lack of interest in men is probably related to two other things. The first one is the hesitation that she experiences during her adolescence about her sexual orientation: she tends to think, by default, that she is a lesbian. The second one concerns those sexual abuses about which she refused to speak—unable to date them, it is difficult to know how they interfere with her history. Nonetheless, it is not surprising that, in this context, her arrival in a technical high school changes the game. "I found myself very ugly at one time, it changed when I moved to another high school and there were not many girls left, and there were a lot of boys and they were interested in me, and that's when I was like, 'What's happening here?' There were a thousand students, there were forty girls, and all the rest were guys. So inevitably, how people look at you inevitably changes how you look at yourself as well, there is your ego that ... [*inhale*] ... well, it's cool!" [face to face].

Élodie thinks that she is in her proper place at this school compared to the social worlds that she had been previously acquainted with. Her situation better fits her expectations: the dominant masculine sociability enables her to depart from the stereotypes of femininity that she readily denounces while, at the same time, enabling easier relations of seduction that make her see her femininity in a better light. Moreover, this situation overlaps with her ambivalence toward her mother's expectations, which she refuses while reproaching herself for this refusal. In this high school, these contradictions are alleviated. She combines academic success with a more masculine mode of socialization.

Within the context of this masculine socialization, the adequacy of her tomboy attitude likely reassures her in the critique of her mother's expectations. It is precisely from the age of eighteen that she says she begins to "dress like a girl," as if this new context provided some distance from the negative image of femininity nurtured since childhood.

"My Little Freedom": Adjustments in Self-Presentation

Displaying oneself is not experienced by Élodie as "natural" and "spontaneous," but *explicitly* as a compromise between various actors: her, her family (especially her mother), and the school environment. Rather than breaking with these actors, she seeks compromises. It is a mechanism that Erving Goffman described as "integrated secondary adaptation."[2] Within the framework of total institutions, this concept refers to the possibility for inmates to deviate from the role assigned to them by the institution, but to do so in such a way as to remain coherent with institutional imperatives.

The issue of clothes often comes back in the participants' narratives. The garments they wear illustrate the stakes that weigh on their bodies. Élodie recounts her difficulties finding a style that avoided conflict with people around her without betraying what she aspires to: an androgynous appearance.

> [Face to face]
>
> ÉLODIE: Heels, miniskirts, it was not appropriate in my middle school. Too small of a town, and even nail polish was prohibited. And in my family, it was even worse, because my parents decreed that we should always have proper attire to go to school. That is, I never went to school in sneakers or in a tracksuit, it was ... the sportiest I could wear was jeans. Otherwise, it was city shoes, and yet for me, the rules were softened somewhat [in relation to my brothers]. That is to say, that I could have a sweatshirt. But at primary school for example ... it was blouse and pullover with the small city shoes, all that stuff, makeup forbidden, nail polish forbidden.
>
> INTERVIEWER: So, the others, at your school, they weren't dressed like you?
>
> ÉLODIE: Oh no. But at the same time their clothes didn't interest me either because.... Seriously, when I arrived at middle school wedge heels were the fashion.... Who would have wanted wedge heels? Certainly not me.

There are three constraints at stake. The young woman had to wear "proper attire" for her parents while not being too sexually suggestive for school. Between these two rules, there is also the more informal one established by her classmates (the wedge-heels fashion, for example), which did not suit her either, mostly because it reinforced the stereotypes of femininity she is so critical of.

[Face to face]

INTERVIEWER: So, you preferred the style that your parents wanted?

ÉLODIE: I had found, a little bit, my freedom in that too. But I still had clothes too big for me and ...

INTERVIEWER: Why?

ÉLODIE: Because I was not very tall, I was all skinny, and I always took things too large for me, I liked it, it was cooler. It was my little freedom.

Élodie finally explains that the dress code instituted by her parents better fits her expectations, by default. As she does not recognize herself in any fashion, the one proposed by her family serves as a refuge: this clothing gives her "neutrality." The only "little freedom" that she seems to care about is the size of the clothes, which she prefers loose. Note that several participants used this strategy. Eva, whom we shall soon meet, also finds freedom by wearing loose clothing. Noémie sees her "rock" style as a good compromise. This androgynous fashion enables her to de-emphasize her femininity while avoiding the cliché of the tomboy.

Let us return to Élodie. Outside of school, the constraints that affect her appearance change.

[Face to face]

INTERVIEWER: And what about ... for example ... makeup, nail polish?

ÉLODIE: No. No makeup, it's when I work and when it's mandatory, that it's written in my contract that I must wear makeup and then that's it. From time to time, to enjoy myself, or to please some people at some party. I'm not a fanatic.

INTERVIEWER: And all the stuff like.... Heels, skirts?

ÉLODIE: [Ironically] Yes, of course, I have already worn some. The first dress I bought was when I was fifteen, and I never wore it. No, the only skirts I wear are my tailored skirts because, same thing, sometimes it's written down in my contract that I am obliged to wear a skirt. I'm more comfortable in pants, so ... it happens to me from time to time, I wear a dress or something [like that].

INTERVIEWER: And your mother now, she tells you nothing about it?

ÉLODIE: My mother wanted me to dress like a girl, to choose girl pants, she took me to shops like Forever 21 or stuff like that … I never found anything to my liking. I was more into baggy pants, extra-large sweats … [*looking at herself*] like today actually …

Élodie says that in the other social worlds, she aims to maintain independence from the constraints imposed by her mother—which seems to radicalize their disagreements. Outside the school setting, she makes fewer compromises with her parents and other norm producers. For example, she only wears makeup or a skirt when it is stipulated in an employment.

The above remarks are not anecdotal. To Élodie, dressing raises important issues. For her, refusing the "femininity" that she is asked to display, means refusing the ready-made path that her mother wishes her to follow. The association of ideas takes place very clearly in her discourse, between the family expectations of success and her gender identity: the whole social imaginary of a way of life (wealthy suburb, etc.) transposes itself to the body. Through gender, this body is made a "battlefield," it embodies the pressures of the different stakeholders, and, eventually, becomes the site of self-aggression.

Antoine: Traumatized by Himself

Tensions regarding gender identity constitute some of the most obvious manifestations of the embodiment of malaise. Antoine, who I meet on the internet, offers another example.

At twenty-two years old, he is undertaking a master's degree in construction. I conduct some interviews with him via instant messaging, but not face-to-face, since at the time he lived in Quebec. His mother is a doctor in public service, the daughter of two high school teachers. His father is a physiotherapist, the son of a railway man and a housewife. He has a brother, who is looking for a job after having completed a master's degree in environmental studies, and a sister who, after a master's degree in chemistry, does one temporary job after another.

Antoine is the youngest of the siblings and is particularly affected by the family atmosphere. Arguments break out daily. There are two opposing camps: he and his mother on one side, his father and his brother on the other. His sister largely stays out of family conflicts. This configuration would explain some of the relational problems he claims to experience (by now, this should not surprise us) and, consequently, his malaise.

Nevertheless, this malaise is characterized by a set of emotions and recurring thoughts, which, according to Antoine, are absent of any links to family life. In some ways, Antoine is reminiscent of Vanessa. On the internet, he describes his sensation of evolving in an imaginary world and regrets that reality is much less thrilling. The distinctness of his experience lies in his conception of sexuality, and in the various practices that result from this. For him, "mental self-injury" coexists with self-inflicted wounds. What he calls "mental self-injury" involves voluntarily placing oneself in situations producing discomfort. For example, he watches pornographic movies in which actresses are put in degrading positions. He says that he spends a lot of time online, reading erotic stories involving children. These images "traumatize" him (in his own words). His practices provoke, sometimes deliberately, panic attacks that he alleviates by injuring himself.

> In addition to participating in a forum dedicated to self-injury, on which he is a moderator, Antoine is part of a discussion forum for sexual abuse victims. Indeed, another of his activities consists in providing help to young women who have been sexually assaulted. While he is probably not directly concerned with these problems, he views this helping role as an obligation, requiring him to be present online and to listen, in confidence, to the life stories of his contacts. "So, what happened was that I was feeling bad, I was 'freezing' myself to be able to bear what the girls I was taking care of said to me, and I was getting too frozen. I was almost a shrink, and on instant messaging it's simpler to unpack problems, even sordid details of sexual abuse" [instant messaging].

One of the young women Antoine helped became his partner in a very special context. They had regular conversations for several months before declaring their love for each other, and entered an internet-mediated romantic relationship. Indeed, at the time, she lived in Canada, he in France. He would have to wait a few more months before he joined her, and settled with her on the other side of the Atlantic.

Where does altruism stop? Where does fascination begin? Between the viewing of pornographic movies that disgust him, and the verbal assistance given to young female victims of abuse, something is undoubtedly played out here at the level of sexuality. Antoine expresses this himself in the following message posted on a forum:

> I am a psychopath of happiness. I don't know how to distinguish the good from the evil, what must make me happy from what must not make me happy.
>
> I will give a comparison/example to illustrate: sex. I'm a psychopath of sex. Before, sex, it was easy: it was wrong. Until then everything was fine. Eventually when one deeply loves a girl, and she wants it, one can make her come, this, it's ok. It's ok because it's the happiness of the other....
>
> So, sex, before everything was filthy or free, was ok. But it appears that one must also take pleasure in it, and there it's hard. Not that it's necessarily hard to take pleasure in it, but what is hard is to know what to do. Before, it was simple, to penetrate a girl was to abuse her, but still it's a little too much, if the girl consents it should be correct. Sodomy, at least, is awful. Ah? There are people who like it and who consent? So, it's okay too? Well, they do whatever they want. Who, me? Ah, me.... But if it's just consenting, it's anything isn't it? I mean, scatophiles are consenting, the actresses even in the most degrading pornos are consenting, everyone agrees, everything is correct.
>
> Who? Me?
>
> I got hurt by seeing all the most degrading movies ever. I spent time on that, but I'm good at searching the internet; I found a lot of these. Are there any that make me fancy the same? No, it's dirty, even the cleanest are dirty, even fellatio is dirty.
>
> Ah yes, no it's true, it's consenting. But everything can be consenting.

Antoine does not provide any clues that would allow us to better understand this point of view. I also fail to ascertain whether he himself experienced events that would make his portrayal of sexual relations a little more comprehensible. Moreover, he does not seem to have been exposed to a redemptive worldview, characteristic of some religious educations for example.

The way in which Antoine expresses himself nevertheless permits us to clarify certain points. He likens all forms of sexual relations to rape, insofar as "everything can be consenting." In other words, nothing is really consented to since sexual practices are fundamentally dirty in his discourse. In the same way that feminist scholars describe the internalization of traditional gender roles by women (educated to hold a submissive posture) and men (socialized to domination), everything happens as if Antoine had internalized male domination against himself, from a guilty perspective.

Let us go further. If, as Antoine says, all sexual relations involve nonconsent and impurity, all men are potential abusers. And "being a man" is precisely one of his difficulties. The negative perception of masculinity manifests itself repeatedly. Remember that one of the examples he gives of "mental-self injury" is "watching disgusting porn movies while being disgusted at being a man." He comes back to the same topic afterward: "There are loads of guys who watch porn movies regularly. Yes, but me, it disgusted me, and I took the most disgusting ones also. . . . It was hardcore, but I'm traumatized. . . . Having simple sexual relationships is not obvious to me." Antoine seems to conceive his condition as a man (in the sense of masculinity) as a negative identity. He presents himself as ambivalent in approaching what he most strongly rejects in this form of masculinity because he would not watch these movies "as a man," but with an eye toward disgusting himself in his masculinity. More specifically, Antoine becomes, for the time of the viewing, what he hates in men.

The guilt associated with this male condition composes a part of his self-hatred and a conflicted relationship to his body that seems necessary in considering self-injuring. At least, this is what the context of his "first real self-injury" may lead us to think. "My first real SI [self-injury], I think, it was a period when I felt bad, and a friend I was in love with had announced to me that her boyfriend had beaten and raped her for five years, I couldn't stand it, I blamed myself, I made myself pay for it, it was not fair that she was suffering. . . . Basically, I was angry at myself for what her boyfriend had done to her" [instant messaging].

By identifying himself with a violent man, Antoine confirms his negative representations of sexuality and masculinity. Is it not in attacking his body that Antoine punishes what he considers problematic in himself? And, is it not in helping sex abuse victims on the internet that he tries to clear himself of guilt, proving that he is not like other men? The association between masculinity and socially negative values recalls Élodie's relationship with femininity. The hatred of the body that results from it, I propose, renders the very idea of self-injury possible.

Tiffany: "You Look Like a Chick"

The association of one's gender with a negative valuation is even more dramatic in the case of Tiffany. I meet her through Clémence—they know each other from a forum. During our first interview on instant messaging, I assume that Tiffany is a woman (as her online presentation looks very "girly"), but Clémence tells me a few days later that in fact "she is a man." I see Tiffany twice in face-to-face meetings. She was born male, was raised to be a man (and presents herself as such most of the time), but likes to dress in a feminine way, and wishes to become a woman, perhaps even, in the future, having gender reassignment surgery. She asks me to "consider her as a woman."

When I first spoke to her, she was twenty-one years old, and was about to complete a technical high school diploma in accounting, working toward a vocational cooperative education program. Her school career is fragmented. She repeated the tenth grade, and completed a health and social vocational training certificate. She then spent two years out of school, looked in vain for work, after which she resumed her studies to obtain her vocational high school diploma.

She began to self-injure at the end of her two years of unemployment.

[Instant messaging]

INTERVIEWER: Can you tell me how it happened for you, SI [Self-Injury]? When did you start, for example?

TIFFANY: It started after these two years when I was out of school, the atmosphere at home was unlivable, failure after failure in the smallest of things I tried, pretty much alone, then, let's say, more around the end [of this period of time], than the beginning.

INTERVIEWER: Okay, what made this atmosphere unlivable?

TIFFANY: Imagine a father who is about to destroy whatever comes under his hand for nothing, screams against everything, besides that, everybody reproaches you for fucking doing nothing, and you, who are anxious about making some move, it doesn't make things better...

But when I speak of reproaches, it is in the morning, in the evening, within each sentence that you hear, for the little you hear.

Her failures, mingled with the reproaches of her father, lead Tiffany to describe the family atmosphere in a very pejorative way. Her father works as a technical draftsman, while her mother stays at home ("always on my back"). According to Tiffany, her parents are "closed-minded ... compared to me, the image that I give."

At first sight, this is a classic situation of academic pressure. Indeed, Tiffany dates the disagreement with her father back to middle school, first as disputes during the sixth grade, and until the ninth grade, where the discord reaches its apogee. "Let's say he was a good student, and he wanted me to be like him. He wanted me to be as good as him, to work the way he did, all evening until he was satisfied," she explains. Tiffany is vague about her grandparents, reluctant to talk about them, and seeming to know very little about them. In short, school pressure contributes to constructing her malaise, both in an external form (through paternal expectations) and in an internalized form, as Tiffany reports being very anxious regarding courses and exams. This anxiety apparently triggered her first self-injury.

But there is another process at stake. Tiffany discovers her desire to be a woman during adolescence.

[Face to face]

INTERVIEWER: How did you discover that you didn't really feel like … a man?

TIFFANY: Well … each time I saw women on the street, with clothes, all that … I wanted to be like that. I didn't talk about it at first, but anyway … I thought it.…

INTERVIEWER: How old were you then?

TIFFANY: It started … um … around thirteen or fourteen… in my head, that was it. [*Silence*].

INTERVIEWER: I guess you felt … uh … I mean in middle school, guys begin to have, we'll say … like "pseudo-virile" discussions!

TIFFANY: [*Laughs*] Yes, yes, that's why … I didn't think like them at all, I was sidelined … and if I had talked about it, I would have been categorized as a freak.…

She began to feminize her style—gradually, so as not to shock anyone. The fear of reactions also triggered instances of self-injury. The sensation of being sidelined also increased. Her father's reaction seems to have been the most negative one. Given the high hopes of academic and social success that he placed in his children, Tiffany's dropping out of school challenges his ambitions."My father said to me one day: 'You look like a chick; if I see you one day in the street I won't know you.…' He has his pride and he doesn't want me to give a picture that breaks this pride" [face to face].

In high school, Tiffany's style is openly feminine. From the moment she affirms herself as such, relations with her parents deteriorate. She cuts off contact with her extended family: "I said to them, 'If I come, it's like that [dressed as a woman at a family meal] and not otherwise'; she'll say 'no,' so I don't go." Tiffany remains "masculine" when looking for a job, gradually assessing the degree of tolerance of her successive bosses regarding her gender preference. Despite her willingness to find friends who would be more understanding, she continued to feel rejected at school.

[Face to face]

I've always had a few friends ... but ... I've always had a few friends but among the others ... I was a little ... the scapegoat.... It's just that I didn't want violence, I didn't want all this stuff ... so when there were problems I kept quiet.... In middle school, it was still going ok, I fit into the mold [*ironic*]. In high school I thought I would find better mentalities, but it didn't change ... it's the same kids but bigger, that's all!

The feminization of Tiffany orients her toward solitary activities such as self-injuring, intensively using the internet, and regularly playing video games.

At our second face-to-face interview, she told me that she "gets better" when meeting with people who accept her self-presentation. Apparently, they are into alternative cultures, including Gothic scenes, or those related to rock and metal music. This release from isolation also allowed Tiffany to define her sexual orientation, of which she had no idea before. Tiffany now feels as though she is attracted to women and plans to undergo a gender reassignment operation. A last revealing element of the physical dimension of her malaise: since everything masculine in her body disguises her, she completely disengages herself by depriving herself of sexuality. "I respect people too much to ... go so far ... there. Let's say that, to speak clearly, what I have between my legs I don't want, I can't bear in mind that ... I will do it [sex] with what I have there" [face to face].

Troubles in Gender

Classical approaches to gender show that women tend to receive more injunctions than men regarding their body and appearances.[3] These studies further suggest that the greater incidence of such injunctions lead women to incline toward self-oriented practices, such as self-injury. This explains why most surveys find self-injury more prevalent among women, as the Adlers have demonstrated.[4] What concrete dynamics underlie this general observation?

People are expected not only to be "men" or "women," but to show it on a regular basis, especially by dressing in a certain way. Gendered behavior is then enacted as a moral dressing,[5] subject to negotiations and conflicts when the rejection of gender stereotypes overlaps with a refusal of social positioning. Thus, the stories of Élodie, Antoine, and Tiffany show that the issue of dressing crystallizes their gender questioning. They distanced themselves from their gender socialization. Élodie, for example, who refuses to dress "femininely," according to circumstances, and Tiffany who expresses the desire to change sex. All three participants illustrate the notion of the embodiment of malaise, that is, the identification of their body as the place of their suffering.

In the cases reported above, a recurrent sociological scenario is at play. The family project is expressed through bodily expectations which preside over the display of gender. One of the family members, the self-injurer, refuses this project and associates it with the values of the gender in question itself. The same-gender parent defends some social aspirations for the family, which strengthens the association made between the family project and the self-injurers pejorative understanding of the gender in question. The self-injurer's peer group fuels this association by reinforcing the family project in terms of bodily expectations. This is especially so because the behavior of the same-gender individuals (often due to a social discrepancy) suggests to the self-injurer that displaying their gender would amount to a form of intellectual degradation. In sum, the self-injurer faces a certain socialization setting regarding gender values—and thus bodily values—that reifies a conception of what being a man or a woman would be in the social world. In so doing, these self-injurers view their place in this world as one characterized by exclusion because this world is populated by problematically gendered "generalized others."[6]

Nevertheless, we can unveil some further dynamics at stake in the gendered distribution of self-injury. First, according to Judith Halberstam, ambiguous gender roles ("tomboys" and "effeminate" boys) are tolerated during early childhood.[7] But in adolescence, young people are asked to position themselves in relation to stable gender binaries. That is, they are required to undertake a social display that could explain why it is in adolescence that conflicts about body and gender arise. This is distinct from the mechanical effects of puberty emphasized by psychologists and medical researchers. Second, we know that women are incited more than men to pay attention to their appearance. Some experimental social psychologists have noted that this attention to appearance refers culturally to negative personality traits in women (the superficial woman), whereas for men, bodily capital and supposed intelligence accumulate in the appreciation by others (a handsome and intelligent man).[8] Women are more likely to feel the staging of their gender as a constraint, which exposes them to higher likelihoods of embodying their malaise.

Finally, if certain social configurations produce among some individuals an oppositional construction of their gender, these configurations rely on a more global context. As Butler pointed out,[9] people position themselves in relation to performative gender stereotypes. These include the supposed intellectual superficiality of women and the alleged brutality of men. When one wishes to find other ways to embody one's gender, the paucity of existing alternative models at their disposal must be recognized. I think that the relative unavailability of alternative conceptions of gender, such as those that circulate in proximity to academic discourses such as queer theory, and the relative weakness of more moderate stereotypes available in more conventional discourses regarding gender (a self-confident-but-not-brutal man, a not-superficial-but-aesthetically-minded woman) may not be convincing-enough alternatives for people who find themselves in situations where their gender is at issue. In other words, different constellations of gender performativity models are limited in their accessibility for those individuals experiencing an embodiment of malaise.

They are left alone in a desert of representations.

11 What Some Events Imply

CERTAIN EVENTS LEAD certain individuals to perceive their bodies as the site of their malaise. These events include violence, long-term disabling accidents, or nonconsensual sex. This last example—nonconsensual sex—is most frequently cited by the people I have met. Correspondingly, most statistical surveys indicate a high proportion of sexual abuse victims among self-injurers.[1]

According to psychiatric publications, my own observations in hospital settings, and the comments of some participants, sexual abuses give rise to what I will call a *total explanatory discourse*. That is, everything happens as if the sexual abuse suffices to explain the socially stigmatized affects and conducts of the victims, including their malaise, their atypical behaviors, their sexual preferences, and everything pertaining to intimacy.[2] In other words, if a sexual abuse victim engages in deviant behavior, these will be systematically interpreted as a consequence of the abuse. Thus, most psychiatric articles devoted to self-harm among victims of sexual abuse often focus on this causal link between trauma and self-injury. In the observed hospitals, I had the impression that the patients who had been abused were subjected to less thorough reflections among staff members, as if the staff already knew the essential elements of their malaise.

Victims also often report sexual abuse as one of the main causes of self-injury. Mentioning the abuse makes it possible to justify a stigmatized practice, making it a more legitimate means of presenting one's self-injury to a sociologist. It is true that this type of event is considered to be among the most violent in our societies, which even leads to some signs of guilt among those who are not victims, such as Stéphanie: "I feel like I'm complaining for nothing … my family has money … and I've not been raped."

In considering the relation of sexual abuse and self-injury, I do not intend to deny the suffering of victims. On the contrary, the aim of this reflection is to avoid reducing them to being only victims, in which case we would already have understood everything. This distance is all the more necessary as the difficulty of defining sexual abuse—when a situation is ambiguous—is compounded by the difficulty victims experience in recalling the circumstances and nature of their abuse, especially when it took place during childhood. Psychiatrists well know that some of their patients fantasize about forced relations. But in all cases, fantasized or not, these events have a considerable impact on the trajectories of the abused individual, through a powerful discourse[3] that amplifies the social significance of having suffered sexual abuse.

I will therefore consider sexual abuses as encompassing actual bodily events, explanatory discourse, and types of sexual relationship whose consequences are socially constructed as being among the most severe on individual self-feeling. These bodily events provoke individuals to redefine the way in which they see themselves, and the way others see them.

Two examples will allow us to study this process. As the family framing appeared to be the most important feature in the stories of participants who reported sexual abuses, I will contrast the case of Benoît (whose family seems to provide him with no support at all), with that of Eva (who benefits from strong family support).

Benoît: The Culture of Silence

Benoît is sixteen years old. I contact him through the internet and we meet for a single interview in a cafe. He is not comfortable during the conversation. He seems divided between the desire to have his malaise acknowledged, and a reluctance to talk about intimate events, which is ultimately why he will refuse a second interview. His father, after studying masonry (probably in secondary vocational training), worked for a few years as an office worker and found himself unemployed for six months. He then decided to create a small business in real estate, which he currently runs. Benoît's mother worked as a psychiatric nurse until she was twenty-six years old, when she decided to leave the workforce, apparently to devote more time to her children's education. She then accumulated several small jobs before becoming the secretary of her husband's company. Benoît has two elder brothers: Victor, twenty-seven years old, is a postal worker, and Jonathan, twenty-four years old, works temporarily in the family business. Both had had a chaotic school career, repeating grades, taking sabbaticals, and changing majors.

Benoît very clearly identifies the source of his malaise and the context in which he carries out his self-injuries. According to him, it is the family situation. The teenager said he is the "jack of all trades," having to deal with the majority of household chores and receiving, in return, nothing but belittling, mockery, and a manifest lack of interest from his parents and brothers.

[Face to face]

INTERVIEWER: So, it's not a great atmosphere in your family?

BENOÎT: Yes, uh ... no. Basically, since my eleventh birthday, it's me who does everything at home; well, not everything ... I don't iron, and I don't do laundry, for example. I did the cooking, the dishes, the housekeeping until I was thirteen, and then they started. I did everything, my parents did nothing, and neither did my brothers. One day the youngest of them was having fun calling me "the dog," and it made my parents laugh! Everyone, so they got used to calling me that ... it's not great.... While my two other brothers are the darlings, they have the right to everything.

It is difficult to understand this configuration, symbolized by a pejorative nickname ("the dog"), although the nickname might have a humorous connotation for the other family members. According to Benoît, the behavior of his parents sometimes amounts to neglect.

[Face to face]

Since they [his brothers] have left the house, everyone is doing their own dishes, everyone has their own life, I don't eat the same as they do so ... what I feel now is, "We don't care about you." For example, today I will go home, Victor, my brother, will take me home ... there they have already left for their weekend; it's like that every weekend. They leave me fifty euros for grocery shopping. There are no shops in the village, so if you don't have a driver's license ... so I don't have anything to eat on the weekends, I mean I have pasta ... it's like that all the time.

In this atmosphere, it was quite logical that Benoît's self-injury began after a family meal. The manner in which Benoît describes his father's attitude in public reveals something of the hatred inspired in Benoît by his situation.

[Face to face]

BENOÎT: My dad makes me ashamed, often when we are eating with friends or with others, well I'm ashamed.

INTERVIEWER: What is it ... his way of being?

BENOÎT: Yes, it is ... I don't know how to say it ... [*With a tone expressing contempt*] I mean he's clowning around, he acts like a moron during the meal. When he speaks seriously for example ... no, he never agrees with others, he's always the only one who disagrees when talking about anything, about religion, about politics. And, so it is always....

When his mother discovers Benoît's scars, a few days after his first self-wound, she seems indifferent to him: "In the days that followed, my mother saw, she said to me: 'You're dumb, you did it to be fashionable, you have no reason,' etc." This reaction was all the more unexpected for Benoît, as he thought that as a former psychiatry nurse she would show more understanding and empathy.

"You Could Have Told Me Before"

Benoît struggles to understand the reasons behind his marginalization in the family. The indifference that he perceives in his parents leaves him confused even if a few hypotheses come to his mind.

[Face to face]

INTERVIEWER: Compared to your brothers, why do you feel less regarded?

BENOÎT: I don't know, it's always been like that. There is ... I don't know, there are several assumptions, I was perhaps not desired. And, my two brothers were born with a two-year gap; I am eight and ten years [away from them], so ... I know that my mother, before me, she miscarried.

Even if, as Benoît hypotheses, this could explain some of the impetus for his parents' behavior, we cannot be certain. Benoît also attributes some part of his malaise to the memory of being touched sexually when he was a child by his brother and a "friend."

[Face to face]

INTERPRETER: And, it dates back to when?

BENOÎT: With my brother, it was on vacation, for a week I slept with him and every night ...

INTERPRETER: At what age?

BENOÎT: I was eight, so he was sixteen. And it was the same every
evening ... actually, I went to bed earlier, since I was eight, and
I've always had problems sleeping ... and he went to bed an hour,
two hours later, and he thought I was sleeping and he touched
me.... [*Moment of silence*].

INTERPRETER: Do you remember it from that moment?

BENOÎT: No, I remembered after. And after that, he kept doing it,
when we got home, I suppose ... until I was eleven. And with my
best friend, it was ... it started at six, he's the same age as I am,
well six months older, so it started at six, or seven, or eight, and
after ... at twelve he asked me again and I told him ... [no], and
since that day I haven't seen him again.

Revisiting these abuses had an atypical effect on Benoît's trajectory.
While he remembers these events without too much discomfort, the beginning of self-injury and the frequenting of internet forums affected him.

[Face to face]

INTERVIEWER: Do you often think about it?

BENOÎT: Let's say that since I cut myself I think of it more. Before,
I mean I don't know, it didn't bother me too much, but when I
started to cut, all my problems, in a way, came back ... and by
going to the forum, reading stories, all that, it has moved me and
it sank me back again....

After a while, he decided to tell his mother. She already suspected
the story with his childhood friend Alexis, but, again, reacted strangely
when he told her about what happened with his brother.

[Face to face]

INTERVIEWER: Your parents, I mean your mother, when she learned
about it, what did she do?

BENOÎT: My mother knew, because when I told her, she told me, "I
know what Alexis did to you," my best friend I mean; she said to
me, "You could have told me before." Because basically, overnight
I stopped talking to him, and my mother never knew why. And
I told her every time, "I'll tell you when I'm ready, I'll tell you
someday," and that's it.... In the village, there is a rumor that my
best friend had abused children, so she assumed that.... It may
have happened, she was wondering why, she imagined the worst,
and ... so she told me about my best friend, and I said, "well, also,

Victor [his brother]. There were also things with Victor." And she basically said, "I've just understood something," but that's all ... it's a little weird....

The way in which Benoît's mother receives this news sheds light on the culture of silence prevailing in his family. If his brother's actions were suspected by other family members, they did not provoke any reaction or empathy. Besides, the teenager has never spoken to Victor about the abuse: Victor still imagines that these abuses are known only to himself. In this context, Benoît feels the anguish arising from the sensation of not understanding what is at stake, and above all, of not being able to explain this law of silence. He suspects family secrets, elements that he is unable to understand, for why his parents and brothers put him in the uncomfortable role of "the black sheep."

This incomplete history shows that the experience of sexual abuse is inseparable from the reception of this information within the family. We have already seen this with Louise, who, having been abused by her grandfather during childhood, runs up against the indifference of her parents. In both cases, when self-injury begins and becomes potentially visible, parental indifference persists. In fact, as self-injury threatens at any moment to break up the (superficial) family unity sought by the parents, to reveal sexual abuse would lead to the designation of a culprit within the family, and the incrimination of all the others, complicit by their silence.

Eva: Sexualization and Desexualization

Eva's story is very different from that of Benoît. I meet this twenty-three-year-old woman for the first time in November 2008. Her hand is in a plaster cast: she broke it by hitting a tree. I did a second interview with her a few months later. Eva is very inclined to talk, the sociological approach prolonging both her psychological follow-up and her literary project. She published an autobiographical book describing her malaise and, more specifically, the sexual abuse of which she was a victim.

Her parents experienced some upward social mobility. Eva's mother grew up in a farmers' family. She studied psychology at the master's level before working as a school psychologist. She then became director of a day nursery, and currently runs a youth center. Eva's father is the son of a postal worker, and a housewife. After completing a vocational high school diploma, he was hired as a technician in a public telecom company, a job that he still holds today. Eva is an only child. Unlike the majority of the participants, she expresses no particular resentment toward her parents.

She describes her early life as relatively happy. "I was fine, a very good pupil, very sociable, all very good," she summarizes. But during her middle school years, some early manifestations of malaise begin to disturb her. "I was in seventh grade. I had tried to hang myself, because I had a bad grade and I was loudly yelled at by my parents; while I thought it was a little exaggerated since I really had, always, very good grades, and I had just had a bad one, and here we go..." [face to face].

These manifestations worsened in the following years. Eva began self-injuring in the ninth grade and provided us with a particularly interesting account of the evolution of her practice, which is worth quoting at length:

[Face to face]

In ninth grade, I began to cut myself, to hit myself a bit, but to cut myself mostly, and nobody knew it. That's when I did it a little on my face, trying to call for help ... but I found so many excuses that eventually people couldn't guess. And in tenth grade, everything was more or less ok, and it is when I came back in eleventh grave, that's when I began to have some trouble in going to class ... it started like that, in fact. So, the first time I couldn't work at home so ... because I stayed in my room and instead of working, I cut myself so I didn't advance [my schoolwork]. So, I ran away for the first time, just for one night, I had not slept the whole night, it was in November, in a forest.... And to skip an exam actually ... and so I missed it, and then there was a second exam that I wanted to miss by telling my parents that I was cutting myself ... and they didn't react that much, but still, I managed to miss the exam and there it is, it happened like that, little by little I missed the classes. I was cutting myself in high school, no one knew except a teacher who somehow took me under her wing, my referent teacher. And after a while, she said to me "No, it's no longer possible, you have to stop going to school," because I was coming to classrooms with my arms covered in blood, people weren't seeing it because I ... I am discreet. But, I was wiping the blood on the table ... it was a little gory. So I stopped, I ... my parents didn't know what to do anymore, so I was hospitalized, I was sixteen years old, in pediatrics, I didn't stayed long because I still appeared to be happy. Everything was going well in my life, I mean I had good grades at school, I had friends, I had relatives who loved me, who supported me, who socialized me, and all that.... So, I didn't get why, I didn't know. So, there I started to see a psychiatrist and every time he got me back to the hospital because I was hurting myself. And that's it, it has been worse and worse. At the beginning, I made small cuts, and I needed to do it stronger and stronger.... And given that, in addition, at the hospital one of the first times in pediatrics, the psychiatrist asked me to show my arm to him and he said to me, "Oh well, it's ok, you don't have many scars!" and so I understood it like, "When you'll have more, you'll be taken seriously," and so I started to cut myself even in the hospital, all that, and it got worse like that. After that, I made my first "official" suicide attempt, official because there were others before but they remained hidden.

Eva gradually commences an irregular lifestyle, mixing schooling interruptions, small jobs, hospitalizations, self-injury, and eating disorders. Most hospitalizations are in the psychiatric ward, though she was at times hospitalized in the general ward, because her cuts regularly required stitching. Eva finally acquired a form of stability by choosing to train as an ambulance officer. It is at this point, she says, that she came to understand many of the reasons for her malaise.

Tough Memories

[Face to face]

During all this time, I was saw shrinks once a week, mostly psychiatrists. And it had been a year since I had a psychoanalyst, and in fact, there, there were memories that came back to me, that I had repressed, abuses when I was eight, they lasted two months. And so, sure, it's not pleasant to remember but ... well, first, it came gradually so I didn't take it all directly ... since at the beginning ... it's still serious ... but it was less serious than I thought. And so at the same time it did me good, because in the end I knew that there was something, I didn't know what, I didn't know with whom, I didn't know at all. But I could see that I was afraid of men, that they mustn't approach me when I was not well. Anyway, everyone suspected that.

The events of which she speaks euphemistically were a series of sexual abuses that her accordion teacher committed when she was a child. As she progressively recalls the instances, she goes back and forth between her hospitalizations and her ambulance work. Although she says that she self-injured less from the moment she remembered the abuses, the severity of her wounds increases.

The manifestations of her malaise will now closely follow the legal procedure she initiates against her former offender.

[Face to face]

[The arrest of the accordion teacher] It was about September 2007. And so it was great for me, because I said to myself, "That's it, things are moving ahead." Everything took a little time to be set up since the complaint.... A confrontation was about to happen, so I was happy, I mean, it may seem odd but in my head, it was thirteen years since I had seen him, he was crazy ... so, I wanted to see him again and to see how he was, because he had grown old ... he was seventy-five years old. [He threatened to commit suicide during his time in custody], so he was released. And well, there I was good, I moved to St. Malo, I settled very quickly, in two weeks it was done, I found the ambulance work, I started two weeks after that, perfect. And I may have been working for about two weeks before I was summoned [by the police] for a psychological assessment, so I said to myself, "That's great," I was really in great shape. And then, my mother received a phone call saying that, like that the assessment had been cancelled, so uh ... and in fact we learned that he was dead. And since we just found out he was dead, I told myself that he probably shot himself because, as he told the cops, "Anyway, I'm screwed up, so I'm gonna commit suicide."

The death of her offender plunges her back into depression. Self-injury intensified, coupled with hospital stays. She decided to try to write her autobiography and find a publisher. She tells me why she had her hand broken during our first interview.

[Face to face]

And so it goes well except that Saturday was the one year anniversary of the suicide of my aggressor, and that's when I broke my hand. In fact, it was because I started a civil procedure to be recognized as a victim and to be compensated ... and so I was received in court about a month ago, and then I found myself alone when I left the court, I didn't know who to call, I didn't know what to do. And so that's when I started to hit my hand. I went in the woods, and I hit myself and it lasted for a month like that until last Saturday; I had been hitting myself every two or three days, actually. And actually I had the obsession to break it. So, when I was fine I said to myself ... "It's completely

silly because it's gonna be super annoying to have my hand broken" ...
and when I wasn't well I had to break it ... and I knew I would get
there because every time I have had obsessions like that, of self-injury,
I don't know, of doing something to myself, I've always done it, and
so Saturday I was more upset than usual, so there we go, I succeeded.

Eva finds herself in the opposite situation as Benoît, since she
focuses her attention on her desire for justice. Eva wants her former
offender to be tried and convicted, and she wants to be compensated
and officially recognized as a victim, while Benoît retreats into a silent
and lonely fatalism. The difference in reaction is surely due to the status
of the aggressor. For Benoît, the abuser is a family member (in addition
to his childhood friend). This is not the case for Eva who can initiate
legal procedures without the family image being brought into question.
For Eva, being a victim does not entail designating a culprit among her
loved ones. Her parents provide her substantial moral and material support, which may explain why she does not regard them as producers or
contributors to her malaise. This is unlike almost all the other participants who attribute to their family some degree of contribution to their
malaise. We can also hypothesize that Eva's parents relaxed the academic pressure they imposed on her before her difficulties began. Before
Eva disclosed to her parents the abuse she had suffered, she described a
certain manifestation of malaise somewhat directly connected to the
pressure exerted on her schooling by her parents.

Moreover, she does not limit herself to parental support. She attends
a victims' association that provides her with additional collective support, likely supporting Eva's managing and dealing with her story. The
publication of her autobiography appears to be the culmination of this
recognition process. All the more so, she said, since those who buy
her book are mostly locals able to discern her real identity despite the
pseudonym.

As a result, Eva is more willing than Benoît to talk about her bodily
sensations and how she has considered her body since she began to self-
inflict wounds. Eva's associative, familial, and judicial supports offered
her a vocabulary and set of rhetorical tools to describe her experience.
She willingly accepts my proposal for a second interview. She can thus
come back to her trajectory through the different perceptions that she
has had of her body.

[Face to face]

Sometimes when I damaged my body I said to myself: "Anyway you don't care, it's not your body, you'll have another … when you'll get better, you'll have another body.…" I mean I was almost saying this to myself. Afterward, of course, I said to myself: "Well no, your body, you'll always have it …" but almost unconsciously … but a little consciously also sometimes … I thought … "No, it's not your body, so you don't care about hurting it, you spoil it, and so what?" So it was the period when I started to eat anything and everything, to get fat, to get fat, and then one day I said to myself … anyway my body, well I was not obese, I was chubby, I said to myself … "I could never accept it like that so.…" But that, it wasn't the time when I made myself vomit, it was more recently … about a year ago. And I said to myself, "No, maybe someday I can accept it like that, but not for now." I said to myself, "Well, so I have only one thing to do, it's losing weight." This is the first thing … the first thing that came to me. And so I took my time, I really took things seriously and now I've lost weight, I already feel better, much better. I also managed to take more care of myself, trying to improve my look a little. I even went one day to do a facial … something I'd never do before, you see. And there too, I dressed very badly at the time, really … at the time, hippie-like it was still ok, it was still ok … and at other times it was really like pants, but kind of, I was a size thirty-eight, I was wearing a forty-two, and loose, wide T-shirts.

The consequence of sexual abuses on her body image seems quite straightforward. The detachment that she operates between "her" and "her body," which would not "really belong" to her ("it's not your body"), is evoked as a consequence of the dispossession that her aggressor has made her live. Sometimes she even perceives the physical sensation of her abuser's hands on her skin, a sensation from which she can detach herself through self-injury.

A Trip to Canada

But other elements come into play. A trip to Canada provoked a real break:

[Face to face]

I remember having wanted to do it [self-injury] actually at the beginning of the ninth grade, I mean during the holidays, the first month of holidays … so in August. I went to Anglophone Canada for three months to learn English and all that. I was very close to my parents, also, and I said to myself, "I must succeed in living without them." Finally, I wasn't feeling that good, so it didn't go very well. And that's when I ... I remember the first time, I remember bumping my head, and I remember, I was looking for something to cut myself with, but I didn't know what, I mean I didn't know the name of the thing [self-injury]. And it was really on my way back from Canada that I really started. So, at first they [her parents] thought it was because of Canada and now, after all this time, I realize it was the trigger but not the cause. But it's true that it was the trigger.

This journey tells us about the emergence of the malaise. The description that Eva provides of the different social environments frequented before, during, and after this trip is revealing of the shift to a more affected state.

[Face to face]

INTERVIEWER: [On your return to France] Have you kept a lot of friends?

EVA: Yes, but not the same at all. I lost them a bit, but, in fact, when I came back from Canada, I was very self-effacing. Before, I was kind of the group leader, and when I came back I was self-effacing, I didn't participate much anymore. I think I had matured all of a sudden ... yes, I had too much to do, because my family in Canada didn't care too much about me, so I had to fend for myself. I managed on my own. So these friends [before the trip] I didn't speak to them anymore, during the breaks I no longer spoke to them, so as a matter of fact, in tenth grade I said myself, "Oh shit, do I join them?" ... or do I stay with people who were in my class that I knew a little, that I liked much less ... but I started a new thing actually.

To understand this "new thing," we must look at Eva's relationships with those around her. Like many other participants, she says that she felt a discrepancy with her peers very early on, a discrepancy caused by the divergence of their interests. From primary school onward, she felt more mature, interested in more intellectual topics of conversation.

[Face to face]

EVA: I was a little different, let's say, yes a little bit I felt that they [my classmates] didn't always understand me. I explained things to them.... [*Mimicking*] "But if it's not so complicated!"

INTERVIEWER: On the level of interests, for example?

EVA: Interests, yes, for example ... there was a time when there were problems in Rwanda and all that ... and so my damn parents talked to me about it ... well, not a lot, but they talked about it anyway. And the others absolutely didn't care at all. And I didn't understand that.

During her middle school years, this feeling of discrepancy diminishes. She says that during this time, there was "no issue." Eva recounts a successful integration into her school, but this smooth integration ends on her way back from Canada. At that moment, she rediscovers a feeling of difference, which she illustrates through the example of fashion sense.

[Face to face]

INTERVIEWER: You were what style of schoolgirl at middle school?

EVA: I dressed anyhow. I didn't pay any attention to my style, it was catastrophic, it was kind of what I could arrive at.... After I had a little trouble in the day because I realized that it didn't make sense at all: tracksuit pants with shoes like Doc Martens, well, that stuff.... Really, I didn't care at all, actually.

INTERVIEWER: And your parents were not trying to tell you [to dress better] ...?

EVA: No. But, it was after I went to Canada for three months, and actually, there, it was just the opposite ... well, it wasn't at all like in France! Because my middle school girlfriends in France, they were the same, they didn't pay too much attention to their style or anything.... While in Canada, they were already ... they were younger than me but they wore small tank tops, sexy things and everything ... and that's when I started to pay a little more attention, because I was really out of step with them there. So ... I said to myself, "Maybe we must do something!"

During her stay across the Atlantic, Eva decides to "sexualize" her style. "I had to buy some clothes there," she says. But, when she went back to France, she did not seem to maintain this momentary attraction to "feminine" styles. On the contrary, she says that she somehow took refuge in associating with a very studious circle of friends, far away from the preoccupations of style and trendiness.

[Face to face]

INTERVIEWER: What kind of people were they [her new friends in high school, when she came back from Canada]?

EVA: They were two doctors' daughters, who didn't party, who didn't laugh very much, who were, rather, about school, school, school. Yes ... not funny! Not the kind of girls you're having fun with, just talking about school.

INTERVIEWER: The girls you knew from middle school [before her trip] they weren't the same?

EVA: Yes, they were more of the bon vivant [a sociable and luxurious individual] type.

INTERVIEWER: But they also came from quite a privileged background?

EVA: Less so. Anyway, in the middle school where we were, most of the people came from a milieu, well, not super-privileged, but in Calais there were two middle schools. There was the one that was next to the peripheral districts, not the big peripheral district either [implying with not much issue]. And ours, it was more people who owned houses. But we were not ... more like modest middle-class, like my parents. There, it was a bit strange, I found myself in eleventh grade with four doctors' daughters and fortunately, I mean fortunately.... There was with me a girl who was a farmers' daughter, so the both of us were a bit out of step. I haven't kept many friends from high school though, only the farmers' daughter actually.

Eva moves from a circle of friends composed of funny middle-class schoolgirls to more serious high-school students from the upper classes, although she seems somewhat annoyed by the sobriety of these studious physicians' daughters. This change coincides with the transformation of her behavior, which she describes in reference to her trip to Canada. While she previously saw herself as being very sociable, Eva now feels timid and discreet. She no longer knows which personality suits her. Her friend, the farmers' daughter, becomes an accomplice with whom she shares this feeling of discrepancy toward others.

These changes in Eva's circle of friends and behavior underlie a desire to avoid the sexualization of social relations. During this high school period, Eva is unsure of her sexual orientation. She expresses a feeling of looming discomfort in the presence of men. Unlike her former middle school friends (the "bons vivants") and her Canadian acquaintances (the "sexy" girls), her new friends are a cure against the potential sexualization of relationships with other high school students.

[Face to face]

> There was a boy that I appreciated, who I knew from middle school, but I felt that I had to say that there was someone who interested me, because otherwise it would have seemed abnormal. At the same time, the two girls I talked to you about, it was the same; the boys, it was like the first one, she was not going to enter a [sexual] relationship before marriage, and the second one just didn't give a shit either. With them I was undisturbed.

This voluntary celibacy can be interpreted in several ways. Does it arise from the history of sexual abuses, knowing that, at this point in her life, Eva struggles to fully remember them? Is it a simple difficulty related to uncertainties about sexual orientation? Torn between the wishes to blend in (to be attracted to a boy) and to find the orientation that seems natural to her, Eva still hesitates. She got into the habit of frequenting the gay scene.

[Face to face]

> INTERVIEWER: And so, regarding guys ... girls ... where are you about physical attraction now [compared to the first interview]?
>
> EVA: [*Laughs*]. Now, it's still pretty complicated; I'm still single, it's been a while. I would think that I would rather be a lesbian ... but really without any certainty. I keep hanging out in the homo scene because I feel better. I'm not saying that I don't like being in the presence of heteros ... because I was with straight people too, and it was ok as well. But.... Yes I keep saying that I am lesbian; it depends, sometimes I'll say that I am bisexual, but in general I say that I'm lesbian, yes.... I have a lot of gay friends too, so they don't give a fuck, they don't see the woman in me at all, they see the friend, and it suits me very well.

Having gay and lesbian friends seems to prolong this will for desexualization, initiated on her return from Canada. Eva finds herself all the more trapped now as she remembers the abuses of her former music teacher. She does not want these events to play a determinative role in her sexual orientation. Affirming her homosexuality could indeed be understood as a rejection of men resulting from the abuses she suffered. "From the age of sixteen, I really thought I was a lesbian, and it was after that I said to myself, especially when my memories came back, I thought ... it's not so sure, it may be just a way to protect myself actually. So I don't know" [face to face].

The Possible Impacts of Bodily Events

Nonconsensual sex may produce an embodiment of malaise, which is "necessary" in order to resort to self-injury. This same process equally applies to traumatic physical events, such as violent encounters or accidents. Indeed, individual and collective appropriation of the memory of the abuse structures the self-injury trajectory, as this event is likely to be considered as one of the major causes, if not *the* cause, of malaise. In other words, we can hardly know the real effect of these events on the probability to self-injure. We can, however, observe that the intertwining between some bodily events, their appropriation, and their management in certain configurations, seems to directly foster the resort to self-aggressive practices such as self-injury.

In the case of sexual abuses, the position of the offender greatly directs this appropriation. Where the aggressor is outside of the family circle, the victim can more easily mobilize his or her family to garner moral and material support. Moreover, this support in the face of abuse can lead to a softening of the family's endeavor to cultivate a certain image or pursue an upward social trajectory. Thus, Eva had the opportunity to "take her time," to "build herself," to change educational and professional orientations, and so on. Where the aggressor *is* a family member, as it was for Benoît or Louise, the abuses create a dilemma. Either the victim is silent, or the whole family is discredited. Often, in these situations, the way in which the family projects itself socially and manages its appearance is radicalized.

In addition to promoting the embodiment of malaise, these events tend to foster the predisposition to deviance (as developed in chapters 8 and 9). Indeed, for victims, the feeling of being "out of step" partly seems to build on the memory of the abuses. We can even assume that nonconsensual sex and the associated discourses legitimize, in some way, the occurrence of deviant activities. People who have suffered sexual abuse are more exposed to social expectations toward deviance. That is, victims of sexual abuse are expected to develop deviant practices and to act in a deviant manner due to their abuse.

Part II Conclusion:
A Relational Map of Self-Injury

Lᴇᴛ ᴜs sᴜᴍ up the reasoning developed throughout the second part of this book. We began our inquiry by asking the following: by what mechanisms do certain dissatisfactions (often toward family and school) give meaning to self-injury? For the practice of self-injury to be possible, certain dispositions must be developed. That is, during their trajectories, the concerned persons have found themselves in situations where the wounds somehow offer comparative advantages vis-à-vis other practices: first, the perceived need to be discreet in expressing one's malaise; second, feeling predisposed to a form of deviance (either through the feeling of difference or discrepancy with others); and third, being led to consider one's body as something problematic, as the place or site of one's malaise. From these, we might understand how some people can attribute a form of efficacy to a potentially discreet practice, which gives rise to a sensation of transgression, and is deliberately self-aggressive.

Unlike most psychiatric publications that focus on their patients' relationship to "others" or "to the world," I found that there is no single world around the participants. The participants are at the heart of a configuration made up of several figures. By figure, I mean the way in which one represents one or more individuals according to the role they are supposed to play. This would include the roles of father, mother, friend, and so on. The people I met during my research described a kind of relational mapping typically composed of four recurring figures: two within the family, and two outside of it.

In the Family

- "Oppressive" figures. These are the people who carry certain aspirations for the whole family. They both endure these aspirations (because their own social trajectories urge them to perceive their aspirations as symbolically vital) and make others endure them (because, to realize these aspirations, all family members must be involved). This figure is usually embodied by the same-sex parent of the participant, and can be relayed through (or fueled by) other family members, often grandparents.

- "Neutral" figures. These are the people who do not nurture the same aspirations as the oppressive figures, or at least not as intensely, because their social trajectories do not lead them to perceive these aspirations as vital. However, their empathy or withdrawal does constitute a challenge to the oppressive figure, since they leave the oppressive figure to structure the family atmosphere. It is common for the other parent to take on this role. Most of the extended family also usually fall into this category.

Outside the Family

- The normative majority of "insiders." Most participants depict a mass of "normal people," well-integrated "inside the system," who are therefore unable to understand their difficulties. These people are deemed to be intolerant or indifferent toward troubles, deviant behaviors, and any supposedly atypical practices. These individuals, who ultimately constitute the normative configuration of society, consolidate malaise by fostering the anticipation of stigmatization, and by extending the norms of the oppressive family figure outside the family.
- The comprehensive minority of the "outsiders." Some individuals play a more empathic role. They are characteristically presented as outsiders," marginalized people who can understand self-injury without judging, being themselves at the margin, and thus more tolerant than the insiders. They are usually confidant teachers or friends who either share similar social situations (experiencing family conflicts, extreme social mobility, etc.) or are affiliated with alternative subcultures (Goths, gays, etc.). Internet forums and psychiatric hospitals are full of "outsiders."

Again, inspired by the anthropology of witchcraft as proposed by Jeanne Favret-Saada,[1] I would say that, for the participants, the normative force of oppressive family figures echoes that of the insiders, since the expectations of the former are also attributed to the latter. At the same time, neutral family figures and outsiders do not suffice to counterbalance this pressure. In this context, self-injurers are led to stake out a position. They could choose to fulfill the expectations of the oppressive figure, and this is partly what they do. Most participants described adopting some of these expectations (by exerting on themselves similar pressures regarding school performance, for example), although they typically express suffering under the weight of such expectations. They could revolt and choose another system of values; however, we have seen that, paradoxically, they are too attached to the values of the oppressor to do so, and there is no group around them that would help them in following such a path.

What are the alternatives? In principle, the most practical possibility would be to adopt a social posture that combines both respect for the normative expectations of the oppressive figures, and the intimate transgression of these norms. In doing so, to borrow Amy Chandler's formulation, they would respond to "the conflict between a desire for authenticity and the increasing difficulty of embodying, or experiencing an authentic self."[2] At the very least, this posture would enable the possibility of holding on and managing some important issues. How to stage one's gender? How to stage one's success? How to stage one's position? How to stage family unity, and through this, the whole set of aspirations it symbolizes? And how to conceal the refusal of certain expectations?

If only irregularly and partially, it is because self-injury allows one to position oneself within these issues that it is possible to understand self-injury as a practice of social positioning.

Conclusion: A Self-Controlled Youth

We are all urged to keep face in daily interactions and to hold a position in the social world. We are all summoned to show ourselves as men or women, poor or rich, to give the appearance of getting involved in our relationships, to "be here," to be "authentic." Therefore, we are all, in a sense, constricted by our bodies, for our bodies are the interface through which social injunctions pass. This book has dealt with the way in which a minority of individuals face these injunctions: self-injury.

In the same way that anthropologists have called into question the Great Divide, which distinguished the West from so-called exotic societies, it is necessary to question this Great Divide that separates supposedly normal individuals from those considered different due to their supposed pathological behavior, or their "mental disorders." If we bought into this notion of a Great Divide, undergirded by the distinction between so-called pathological and normal individuals, it would have been possible to develop an analysis that assumes a specific mental functioning in self-injurers, and a specific pattern of action. But what would that have been for, if not to reassure those who do not self-injure of their supposed normality? Therefore, in this book, I have set out to study self-injury as a practice denoting a form of positioning that is reasonable in the face of certain social configurations. And the issues that constitute these configurations affect us all: social positioning, gender identity, self-presentation, and so forth.

In what remains of this conclusion, I wish to scale up my analysis by placing self-injury within a broader, historical context. Norbert Elias' notion of the "civilizing process,"[1] provides a vantage point from which to historicize self-injury. According to Elias the emotional economy of individuals in European societies has been transformed following the Middle Ages, where "the lives of the warriors, like that of other people living in a warrior society, are constantly threatened by brutal aggression.... Warriors have the freedom to exteriorize their feelings and passions, they can indulge in wild joys, satisfy their sexual appetites, give free rein to their hatred by devastating everything that belongs to them to one extent or another."[2] But, gradually a civilizing process took place in the West, leading to (among other things) a privileging of self-control over the expression of impulses. Elias writes that today, "the man who is unable to repress his spontaneous impulses and passions compromises his social existence; the man who knows how to control his emotions benefits, on the contrary, from obvious social advantages, and each one is led to reflect before acting on the consequences of his actions. The repression of spontaneous impulses, the control of emotions, the widening of mental space, that is, the habit of thinking about past causes and future consequences of one's acts, are some aspects of the transformation that necessarily follows the 'monopolization of violence' and the 'extension of the networks of interdependence.'"[3] By "monopolization of violence," Elias means that whereas in the Middle Ages, many small seigneuries were constantly waging war with each other, the struggle for hegemony of the feudal lords gradually led to the emergence of wider and more centralized territories. Emerging states claimed a monopoly on legitimate violence. As a result, individuals are increasingly obliged to self-control, partly because violence is regulated by the central government.

By "extension of the networks of interdependence," Elias motions toward the fact that during the Middle Ages, fragmented feudal territories meant that individuals depended on only a small number of people for their survival. Nowadays, we are embedded within a very extensive network of interdependence. We do not know the (very important) number of people on whom we indirectly rely to live.

These two movements explain why contemporary individuals have had to learn to self-control. Because violence is monopolized, and the repercussions of emotional overflows are less manageable as our networks of interdependence have extended beyond our control, individuals have had to develop techniques of self-control.

This leads to a transformation of violence at a symbolic, ritualized level, illustrated in Elias' and Eric Dunning's study on sport.[4] Elias and Dunning show that over the centuries, the pleasure of the athletes and spectators who watch them has shifted. We have traveled from the enjoyment of acts of actual violence (such as killing a person or an animal) to the craze of anticipation and the simulation of this violence (simulating fight, staging death, "playing" violence). We went from gladiator fights to wrestling matches.

Considered in Goffmanian terms, this process implies some significant changes. Most notably, we have seen a rise in the pressure on, and significance of, face work, as a site of significant power, and a concomitant decline in the significance of physical strength and even material possessions. We have further witnessed a shift in the meaning of involvement, as people must keep a distance from certain roles to stay in command of themselves within an interaction. Accompanying these changes is a rise in the significance of embarrassment, for being embarrassed is one of the worst possibilities in such a world of appearances. What is more, Elias' theory allows us to historicize what Goffman tends to portray as relatively universal.

In line with this process, self-injuries are deferred modalities utilized to manage interaction (hurting oneself after the interaction rather than reacting in the moment) and violence (harming one's body rather than being aggressive toward someone else). They perfectly correspond to the nature of contemporary social life depicted by Elias. That is, they are a bodily investment that *represents* subversion more than it presents a *possibility of disturbing* the order.

Dominique Memmi has used this expression, "bodily investment," regarding demonstrators.[5] In the West, it has been a long time since a demonstration seriously threatened to shake the foundations of power. Nobody has been even close to taking control of power since the Second World War. However, protestors continue to represent themselves through a defined set of physical postures. They present themselves bodily, as a popular menace. But, they represent this menace more than they threaten to enact it. Observing this process whereby the ceremonial subversion of power takes precedence over its materiality allows us to better understand Goffman's sociology. Indeed, his recurrent distinction between what is "substantial" and what is "ceremonial" implicitly relies on (and thus depicts) a historical configuration marked by a relative political stability, or, a given stage in the process of civilization.

As they hurt themselves, rather than attacking what they identify as the source of their malaise, self-injurers fall within this process, and in fact, support it. If they stage a threat toward their family, their school, their social milieu, the people around them, it is only their physical integrity that is truly threatened. Living the civilizing process in such a way requires a certain—historically and socially situated—disposition to manage one's mental life (as evinced in chapter 5), the symbols emerging from one's trajectory (discussed in chapter 6), family, school (broached in chapters 7–9), and gender-related issues (considered in chapters 10–11), as matters of self-control.

The relation established by Elias between the management of affects and the organization of power opens many avenues for analysis.

I would first venture to assume that self-injurers—because they say that they self-injure in relation to very individualized emotions (anguish, self-hatred, anxiety, feeling of emptiness, and so forth)—actually experience, in an immediate and pressing way, the backlash resulting from the impossibility of adequately identifying the extent of the network of interdependence that structures their social life. Catherine Lutz has contrasted the perception of emotions "without recipient,"[6] typical of the Western individual, to the approach of the Ifaluks (a small, Pacific island society of a few hundred people), to always address emotions to someone or to a situation. The difference between these two emotional configurations may lie partly in the possibility that the Ifaluks have to identify who they depend on, and are thus required to identify more distinctly which situation their emotions refer to.

Following this suggestion, the historical extension of networks of interdependence around individuals in contemporary societies—recognizable nowadays in the form of globalization, which is aided by communication and information technologies—results in the opposite effect. In other words, it is almost impossible to identify a source of one's malaise and, as a result, Western individuals are made able to feel and express emotions without a cause. The individualization of troubles is generally attributed to the psychological and medical professions, since they have most successfully promulgated representations of an isolated self. Here I seek only to propose the social conditions necessary for such discourse to operate.

Furthermore, it should be noted that self-injury is socially framed through an "ethos of compassion,"[7] a set of sociocultural codes expressing a disposition to listen and attend to the self-injurer's suffering. It is a mechanism of power: the social designation of certain behaviors or of certain populations to be interpreted or taken care of through the register of suffering draws a boundary. The register of compassion provides individuals with a (often exclusive) interpretive grid of their situations and behaviors. Thus, their situations and behaviors are read as the result of their vulnerabilities. These people are encouraged by some social actors to perceive their difficulties through the prism of their own inabilities, their intimate disarray.[8] Compassion thus forestalls and defuses the diffuse claims potentially conveyed by behaviors such as self-injury.

In a society where the bodily maintenance of healthy individuals is subjected to powerful injunctions to self-manage,[9] voluntarily injuring one's body constitutes one of the most elaborate, and extreme forms of self-control, since the injured person transgresses the norm in order to better respect it. This small group of adolescents and young adults who self-injure to manage their anger, disappointment, and feeling of isolation in the social world, embody a radicalized ideal of our civilization.

Hence, against the flow of contemporary worries regarding the excesses of deviants, we have dealt with a minority of dispersed individuals who, under the register of suffering, transgress the order to reproduce it: a self-controlled youth.

Notes

Introduction

1. Bourdieu, "De la domination masculine," *Le monde diplomatique* (August 1998).

2. In this regard, I share the path taken by Chandler, *Self-Injury, Medicine and Society* (London: Palgrave Macmillan, 2016).

3. Steggals, *Making Sense of Self-Harm* (New York: Palgrave Macmillan, 2016).

4. Mauss, *On Prayer* (Oxford: Berghahn, [1909] 2003).

5. According to the classification of Favazza, *Bodies under Siege* (Baltimore, MD: Johns Hopkins University Press, 1987).

6. See for example, Kerr, Muehlenkamp, and Turner, "Nonsuicidal Self-Injury," *Journal of the American Board of Family Medicine* 23, no. 2 (2010): 240–259.

7. The most recent metastudies of self-injury prevalence are due to Swannell, Martin, Page, Hasking, and St. John, "Prevalence of Nonsuicidal Self-Injury in Nonclinical Samples" *Suicide and Life-Threatening Behavior* 44, no. 3 (2014): 273–303, http://onlinelibrary.wiley.com/doi/10.1111/sltb.12070/full. They write that self-injury prevalence is estimated to "17.2 percent among adolescents, 13.4 percent among young adults, and 5.5 percent among adults." Another important source is Muehlenkamp, Claes, Havertape, and L. Plener, "International Prevalence of Adolescent Non-suicidal Self-injury and Deliberate Self-harm," *Children and Adolescent Psychiatry and Mental Health* 6, no. 10 (2012): 2–9. They measure the "lifetime prevalence" of self-injury as being around 18 percent.

8. Whitlock, Eckenrode, and Silverman, "Self-Injurious Behaviors in a College Population," *Pediatrics* 117, no. 6 (2006): 1939–1948; Nixon, Cloutier, and S. Jansson, "Nonsuicidal Self-Harm in Youth," *Canadian Medical Association Journal* 178, no. 3 (2008): 306–312.

9. Bresina and Schoenleberb, "Gender Differences in the Prevalence of Nonsuicidal Self-Injury," *Clinical Psychology Review* 38 (2015): 55–64.

10. Hodgson, "Cutting through the Silence," *Sociological Inquiry* 74, no. 2 (2004): 162–179.

11. Adler and Adler, *The Tender Cut* (New York: NYU Press, 2011).

12. Especially with H. Philips and Alkan, "Recurrent Self-Mutilation," *Psychiatric Quarterly* 35, no. 3 (1961): 424–431. They are much more specific than Karl Menninger's book, *Man Against Himself*, initially published in 1938. We should note that in most historical periods some forms of self-aggressive behaviors can be found, yet these are different from contemporary self-injury, as Steggals, *Making Sense of Self-Harm* also points out. I have published a more detailed historical

exploration of self-injury in this book chapter Baptiste Brossard, "Des automutila-
tions dans l'histoire," in *Proscrire / Prescrire*, ed. Cédric and Hardy (Rennes, France:
Presses Universitaires de Rennes, 2011), 89–102.

13. See Hawton, L. Harriss, S. Hall, S. Simkin, E. Bale, and A. Bond, "Deliberate
Self-Harm in Oxford, 1990–2000," *Psychological Medicine* 33, no. 6 (2003): 987–995;
Kerr, Muehlenkamp, and Turner, "Nonsuicidal Self-Injury," 240–259.

14. W. Walsh and Rosen, "Self-Mutilation and Contagion," *The American Journal
of Psychiatry* 142, no. 1 (1985): 119–120; J. Taiminen, Kallio-Soukainen, Nokso-
Koivisto, Kaljonen, and Helenius, "Contagion of Deliberate Self-Harm Among
Adolescent Inpatients," *Journal of the American Academy of Child & Adolescent
Psychiatry* 37, no. 2 (1998): 211–217.

15. Cawthorpe, D. Somers, T. Wilkes, and M. Phil, "Behavioral Contagion
Reconsidered," *The Canadian Child and Adolescent Psychiatry Review* 12, no. 4
(2003): 103–106.

16. Pommereau, Brun, and Moutte, *L'adolescence scarifiée* (Paris: L'Harmattan,
2009).

17. See for example Mustanski, "Getting Wired," *Journal of Sex Research* 38, no.
4 (2001): 292–301.

18. I have used this method as formalized in France by Beaud and Weber, *Guide
de l'enquête de terrain* (Paris: La Découverte, 2003).

19. This concept is developed in Bourdieu, *Practical Reasons* (Stanford, CA:
Stanford University Press, 1996).

1. The First Time

1. Adler and Adler, *The Tender Cut* (New York: NYU Press, 2011); Best and
F. Luckenbill, *Organizing Deviance* (Englewood Cliffs, NJ: Prentice Hall, 1982).

2. Grange, *Une sociologie de* (Paris: L'Harmattan, 2010), 17.

3. Becker, *Outsiders* (New York: The Free Press of Glencoe, [1963] 2008), 25.

4. Ibid., 42.

5. Emerson and Messinger, "The Micro-Politics of Trouble," *Social Problems* 25,
no. 2 (1977): 121–134.

6. Adler and Adler, *Tender Cut*.

7. Adler and Adler, *Tender Cut*, and Hodgson, "Cutting through the Silence,"
Sociological Inquiry 74, no. 2 (2004): 162–179, highlight the "other-learned" dimension
of self-injury, especially from the late 1990s, Amy Chandler, *Self-Injury, Medicine and
Society* (London: Palgrave Macmillan, 2016), puts emphasis on the lonely reflection
endeavored by self-injurers regarding moral concerns and "authenticity."

8. Chandler, *Self-Injury, Medicine and Society*.

9. This will to "takeover" is, according to Darmon, the first step toward entering an anorexic career: Muriel Darmon, "The Fifth Element," *Sociology* 43 (2009):
717–733.

10. These two expressions refer respectively to A. Cloward, "Illegitimate Means,
Anomie, and Deviant Behavior," *American Sociological Review* 24, no. 2 (1959):

164–176; Bourdieu, *Practical Reasons* (Stanford, CA: Stanford University Press, 1996).

11. Darmon, "Fifth Element," 717–733.

12. See for example Sara Canetto and Sakinofsky, "The Gender Paradox in Suicide," *Suicide and Life-Threatening Behavior* 28, no. 1 (1998): 1–23.

13. Pommereau, "Les violences cutanées auto-infligées à l'adolescence," *Enfances & Psy* 32, no. 3 (2006): 58–71.

14. Miskec and McGee, "My Scars Tell a Story," *Children's Literature Association Quarterly* 32, no. 2 (2007): 163–178. In France, Grange (*Sociologie de l'autodestruction*) observed the growing media outreach of the figure of the self-destructive individual during the 1990s.

2. Toward a Feeling of Dependence

1. Becker, *Outsiders* (New York: The Free Press of Glencoe, [1963] 2008), 25.

2. Reference is made to this pioneer study: Zborowski, "Cultural Components in Responses to Pain," *Journal of Social Issues* 8, no. 4 (1952): 16–30.

3. Laomela, *Le train de la lâcheté* (Jouaville, France: Scripta, 2008).

3. Talking about Self-Injury?

1. Whitlock, Eckenrode, and Silverman, "Self-Injurious Behaviors in a College Population," *Pediatrics* 117, no. 6 (2006): 1939–1948.

2. Adler and Adler, *The Tender Cut* (New York: NYU Press, 2011); Conterio, Lader, and K. Bloom, *Bodily Harm* (New York: Hyperion, 1998); Tyler, B. Whitbeck, R. Hoyt, and D. Johnson, "Self-Mutilation and Homeless Youth," *Journal of Research on Adolescence* 13, no. 4 (2003): 457–474.

3. Bellamy, Roelandt, and Caria, "Troubles mentaux et représentations de la santé mentale," *Études et résultats* 347 (2004): 1–12.

4. Mauss, *The Gift* (London: Cohen, [1950] 1966).

5. Vaux, "Variations in Social Support Associated with Gender, Ethnicity, and Age," *Journal of Social Issues* 41, no. 1 (1985): 89–110.

6. Chandler, *Self-Injury, Medicine and Society* (London: Palgrave Macmillan, 2016).

7. This dimension relates to the "ontological axis" in the frame of his thesis: Steggals, *Making Sense of Self-harm* (New York: Palgrave Macmillan, 2016), chapter 3.

8. Chandler, *Self-Injury, Medicine and Society*, chapter 3.

4. Quitting

1. Lézé, *L'autorité des psychanalystes* (Paris: Presses Universitaires de France, 2010).

2. This is what is shown by Coutant, *Délit de jeunesse* (Paris: La Découverte, 2003).

5. Self-Injury on a Regular Basis

1. Goffman, *Interaction Ritual* (Garden City, NY: Doubleday, 1967).
2. Cooley, *Human Nature and the Social Order* (New York: Schocken, [1922] 1964).
3. Lutz, *Unnatural Emotions* (Chicago: University of Chicago Press, 1988).
4. Goffman, *Interaction Ritual*.
5. Ariès and Duby, *A History of Private Life, Volume II* (Cambridge, MA: Harvard University Press, 1993).
6. Deville-Cavellin, *Automutilation* (Nantes, France: Amalthée, 2005). Excerpt translated by the author.
7. I herein refer to: Hochschild, "Emotion Work, Feeling Rules, and Social Structure," *American Journal of Sociology* 85, no. 3 (1979): 551–575.
8. Walsh, *Treating Self-Injury* (New York: Guilford, 2008).
9. Numerous comparative studies suggest this: Friedlmeier and Trommsdorff, "Emotion Regulation in Early Childhood," *Journal of Cross-Cultural Psychology* 30, no. 6 (1999): 684–711; the synthesis of Gayet has been particularly useful to me: Gayet, *Les pratiques éducatives des familles* (Paris: Presses Universitaires de France, 2004).

6. On the Manners to Ways

1. Hochschild, "Emotion Work, Feeling Rules, and Social Structure," *American Journal of Sociology* 85, no. 3 (1979): 551–575.
2. Douglas, *Purity and Danger* (London: Routledge and Kegan Paul, 1966).
3. Still in the sense of Hochschild, "Emotion Work," 551–575.
4. Thoits, "Self-Labelling Processes in Mental Illness," *American Journal of Sociology* 91, no. 2 (1985): 221–249.
5. Paulme, "Sur quelques rites de purification des Dogon (Soudan français)," *Journal de la Société des africanistes* 10, no. 1 (1940): 65–78.
6. This is similar to what Steggals, *Making Sense of Self-harm* (New York: Palgrave Macmillan, 2016), suggests, but he asserts that self-injury is a "late-modern idiom of personal distress."

Part I Conclusion: Maintaining the Order

1. Balandier, "Réflexions sur le fait politique," *Cahiers internationaux de sociologie* 37 (1964): 23–50.
2. In this sense, this behavior is very close from the "hyperconformist" routine of the anorexics studied by Darmon, Darmon, "The Fifth Element," *Sociology* 43 (2009): 717–733.
3. I refer anew to the theory of practice developed by Bourdieu, *The Logic of Practice* (Cambridge: Polity, 1992). Let us emphasize what Bourdieu calls

"reasonable": it is an alternative to the adjective "rational" (and by extension, to methodological individualism), aimed at posing individual action both as determined and purposely acted. In other words, using this concept does not suggest that self-injury would be reduced to a solely conscious, rational behavior.

Part II: Introduction

1. Evans-Pritchard, *Witchcraft, Oracles and Magic among the Azande* (Oxford: Oxford University Press, [1937] 2002).

2. Favret-Saada, *Deadly Words* (Cambridge, UK: Cambridge University Press, [1980] 2010).

3. I herein allow myself to use the concept of looping effect in a much smaller scale than Hacking did, which is not incompatible with his broader critique of social constructionism. Hacking, *The Social Construction of What?* (Harvard, MA: Harvard University Press, 2000).

4. The most striking historical—and controversial—demonstration of this remaining Ariès, *Centuries of Childhood* (New York: Alfred A. Knopf, 1962). Most arguments proposed in this paragraph endorse the majority of historical and sociological works dealing with Western families. See for instance: Casey, *The History of the Family* (Oxford: Blackwell, 1989). Chambers, *A Sociology of Family Life* (Cambridge, UK: Polity, 2012).

5. This point has been particularly demonstrated in France by the work of Garcia, *Mères sous influence* (Paris: La Découverte, 2011).

6. Sirota, *L'école primaire au quotidien* (Paris: Presses Universitaires de France, 1988).

7. T. Pfeffer and R. Hertel, "How Has Educational Expansion Shaped Social Mobility Trends in the United States?" *Social Forces* 94, no. 1 (2015): 143–180; J. Blanden "Cross-Country Rankings in Intergenerational Mobility," *Journal of Economic Surveys* 27 (2013): 38–73.

8. Naudet, *Entrer dans l'élite* (Paris: Presses Universitaires de France, 2010).

9. Chauvel and Schröder, "The Impact of Cohort Membership on Disposable Incomes in West Germany, France, and the United States," *European Sociological Review* 31, no. 3 (2014): 298–311.

10. Doob, *Social Inequality and Social Stratification in U.S. Society* (London: Pearson, 2013); M. Lee and Kramer, "Out with the Old, In with the New? Habitus and Social Mobility at Selective Colleges," *Sociology of Education* 86, no. 1 (2013): 18–35.

11. This has a lot to do with my PhD supervisor, Florence Weber. See Weber, "Settings, Interactions and Things," *Ethnography* 2, no. 4 (2001): 475–499.

7. The Staging of Discretion

1. This citation is retrieved from a summary of *The Distinction* in Bourdieu, *Questions de sociologie* (Paris: Éditions de Minuit, 1984).

8. At the Origin of "Relational Problems"

1. J. Scheff, *Being Mentally Ill* (Chicago: Aldine, 1966).

2. Initially stamped by Bourdieu, this concept has been particularly developed by Lahire, *The Plural Actor* (Cambridge, UK: Polity, [2006] 2011).

9. The Existential Crisis

1. Bourdieu, *Practical Reasons* (Stanford, CA: Stanford University Press, 1996).

2. I herein wish to elucidate a bridge with Chandler's approach to self-injury in terms of a quest for "authenticity." Chandler, *Self-Injury, Medicine and Society* (London: Palgrave Macmillan, 2016).

3. Activism in the working class has been observed as being a potential motor of upward social mobility by Fossé-Poliak, "Ascension sociale, promotion culturelle et militantisme, une étude de cas," *Sociétés contemporaines* 3, no. 1 (1990): 117–129.

4. Bourdieu, *The Logic of Practice* (Cambridge, UK: Polity, 1992).

5. K. Merton, *Social Theory and Social Structure* (New York: Free Press, 1949).

6. Muel-Dreyfus, *Le métier d'éducateur* (Paris: Éditions de Minuit, 1983).

7. The solitary nature of self-injury is largely developed in Adler and Adler, *The Tender Cut* (New York: NYU Press, 2011), chapter 6.

8. I initially refer to the French context depicted by Beaud and Pialoux, *Violences urbaines, violences sociales* (Paris: Hachette, 2005). But similar observations can be found in the United Kingdom or the United States—see for instance Weis, *Working Class without Work* (New York: Routledge, 1990).

9. On the relationship between emotion and social position, see Foy, Freeland, Miles, B. Rogers, and Smith-Lovin, "Emotions and Affect as Source, Outcome and Resistance to Inequality," in *Handbook of the Social Psychology of Inequality*, ed. D. McLeod, J. Lawler, and Schwalbe (New York: Springer, 2014), 295–324.

10. The stigmatization and double-binds associated with social mobility, particularly in working-class students aspiring to higher education, has been described in several countries, for instance: M. Lee and Kramer, "Out with the Old, In with the New? Habitus and Social Mobility at Selective Colleges," *Sociology of Education* 86, no. 1 (2013): 18–35; Pasquali, "Les déplacés de l' 'ouverture sociale'," *Actes de la recherche en sciences Sociales* 183, no. 3 (2010): 86–105; Granfield, "Making It by Faking It," *Journal of Contemporary Ethnography* 20, no. 3 (1991): 331–351.

11. Beaud and Amrani, *Pays de Malheur! Un jeune de la cité écrit à un sociologue* (Paris: La Découverte, 2004).

12. Paechter, *Being Boys, Being Girls* (Maidenhead, UK: Open University Press, 2007); Adler, J. Kless, and Adler, "Socialization to Gender Roles," *Sociology of Education* 65, no. 3 (1992): 169–187.

13. Pialoux, "Alcool et politique dans l'atelier," *Genèses* 7, no. 1 (1992): 94–128.

10. What Gender Represents

1. Chandler grandly elaborates on the corporeality of self-injury, placing it in the frame of contemporary discourses regarding the body, identity, and medicine. Chandler, *Self-Injury, Medicine and Society* (London: Palgrave Macmillan, 2016).

2. Goffman, *Asylums* (New York: Anchor Books, 1961).

3. I refer to gender research in general, as presented by Connell, *Gender*, 2nd ed. (Cambridge, UK: Polity, 2009).

4. Adler and Adler, *The Tender Cut* (New York: NYU Press, 2011), 200–203.

5. Butler, *Gender Trouble* (New York: Routledge, 1990).

6. The use of the notion "generalized other" is, of course, derived from Mead, *Mind, Self, and Society from the Standpoint of a Social Behaviorist* (Chicago: University of Chicago Press, 1934).

7. Halberstam, *Female Masculinity* (Durham, NC: Duke University Press, 1998).

8. A review of evidence has been done by Amadieu, *Le poids des apparences* (Paris: Odile Jacob, 2002).

9. Butler, *Gender Trouble*.

11. What Some Events Imply

1. For example Whitlock, Eckenrode, and Silverman, "Self-Injurious Behaviors in a College Population," *Pediatrics* 117, no. 6 (2006): 1939–1948.

2. Another (complementary) way of approaching this issue is offered by Steggals, whose analysis examines traumas as a discursive condition of possibility of self-injury (Chapter four, "The Aetiological Axis"). Steggals, *Making Sense of Self-Harm* (New York: Palgrave Macmillan, 2016).

3. This relation between power and "sexual stories" is best developed by Plummer, *Telling Sexual Stories* (London: Routledge, 1995).

Part II Conclusion: A Relational Map of Self-Injury

1. Favret-Saada, *Deadly Words* (Cambridge, UK: Cambridge University Press, [1980] 2010).

2. Chandler, *Self-Injury, Medicine and Society* (London: Palgrave Macmillan, 2016), 14.

Conclusion: A Self-Controlled Youth

1. Elias, *The History of Manners, The Civilizing Process*, vol. 1 (Oxford: Blackwell, 1969); *State Formation and Civilization, The Civilizing Process*, vol. 2 (Oxford: Blackwell, 1982).

2. Elias, *State Formation*.

3. Ibid.

4. Elias and Dunning, *Quest for Excitement* (Leicester, UK: Blackwell, 1986).

5. Memmi, "Le corps protestataire aujourd'hui," *Sociétés contemporaines* 31, no. 1 (1998): 87–106.

6. Lutz, *Unnatural Emotions* (Chicago: University of Chicago Press, 1988).

7. This notion is borrowed from Fassin, "Souffrir par le social, gouverner par l'écoute, une configuration sémantique de l'action publique," *Politix* 73 (2006): 137–157.

8. This collective understanding of self-injury through the prism of compassion and psychology somehow meets with what Steggals, *Making Sense of Self-Harm* (New York: Palgrave Macmillan, 2016), chapter 5, names "the pathological axis," one of the discursive conditions making self-injury possible, according to his analysis.

9. Armstrong, "The Rise of Surveillance Medicine," *Sociology of Health & Illness* 17 (1995): 393–404.

Index

BAPTISTE BROSSARD, a French sociologist, is Lecturer at the Australian National University.

CPSIA information can be obtained
at www.ICGtesting.com
Printed in the USA
LVHW111722120919
630868LV00006B/918/P